The
HIDDEN

of the
LAKE DISTRICT & CUMBRIA

Acknowledgements

The Publishers would like to thank the following for their assistance in the production of this book: Elaine, Deborah and Kelly for Administration. Graham and Timothy for Production. Bob, Julian, Claire, Rick and Sam for Research Joanna, Gerald and Graham for Writing. Sarah, Les, Graham and Timothy for Artwork., Simon at Scorpio for the maps.

Full page line drawings are by Ted Gower and Albert Simister

OTHER TITLES IN THE HIDDEN PLACES SERIES
Ireland
Scotland
North Wales
South Wales
The Welsh Borders
Northumberland & Durham
Lancashire, Cheshire and the Isle of Man
Yorkshire
Devon and Cornwall
East Anglia
Somerset, Avon, Glos, Wilts.
Dorset, Hants, I.O.W.
Thames & Chilterns
The Heart of England
The South East
(ORDER FORM AT BACK OF BOOK)

© M & M Publishing Ltd. 118 Ashley Rd .Cheshire. U.K. WA14 2UN

Foreword

The Hidden Places Series

This is an established collection of travel guides which covers the U.K and Ireland in 16 titles.

The aim of the books is to introduce readers to some of the less well known attractions of each area whilst not ignoring the more established ones.

We have included in this book a number of hotels, inns, restaurants, various types of accommodation, historic houses, museums, and general attractions which are to be found in this part of the country, together with historical background information.

There is a map at the beginning of each chapter with line drawings of the places featured, along with a description of the services offered.

We hope that the book prompts you to discover some of the fascinating "Hidden Places" which we found on our journey, and we are sure the places featured would be pleased if you mentioned that our book prompted your visit.

We wish you an enjoyable and safe journey.

THE HIDDEN PLACES
OF
The Lake District & Cumbria

CONTENTS

CHAPTER ONE

Kendal and the Cumbrian Dales

Barbon Beck, Nr Kirkby Lonsdale

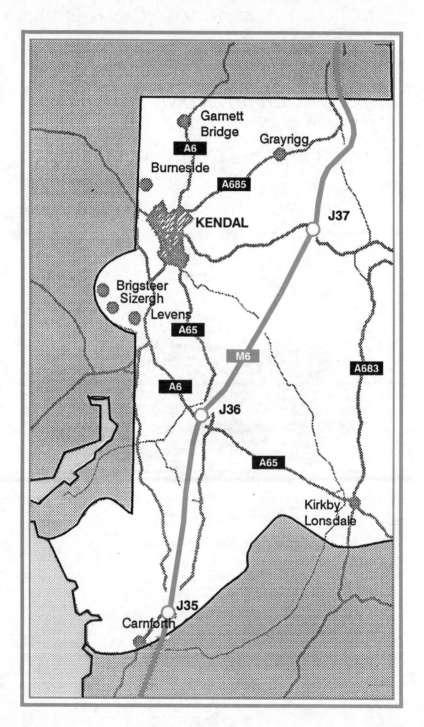

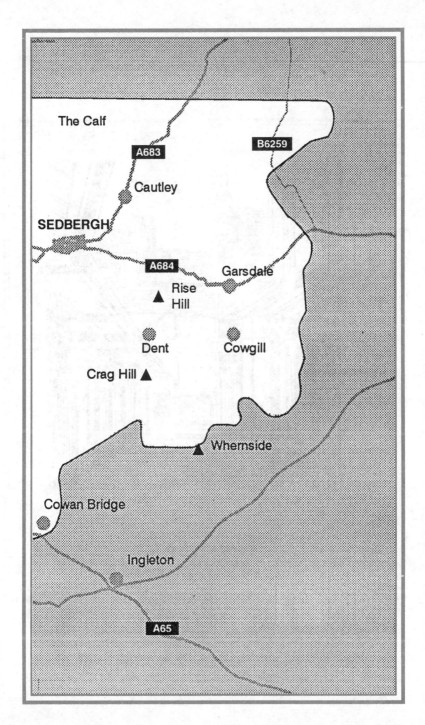

Kendal's 'Yards'

CHAPTER ONE

Kendal and the Cumbrian Dales

KENDAL, an ancient town in the valley of the River Kent, was once one of the most important woollen textile centres of Northern England. The Kendal woollen industry was founded in 1331 by one John Kemp, a Flemish weaver. It flourished and sustained the town for almost 600 years until the development of competition from the huge West Riding mills in the Industrial Revolution of the 19th century.

The town was also famous for its Kendal Bowmen, skilled archers clad in Kendal Green cloth, whose longbows were made from local yew trees on the nearby limestone crags. It was these men who fought so decisively against the Scots at the Battle of Flodden Field in 1513.

Kendal has royal connections too. Katherine Parr, the last of Henry VIII's six wives, lived at **KENDAL CASTLE** in the 16th century before she became Queen of England. Today its ruins, high on a hill overlooking the town, locate one of the original Roman camps that guarded the route to the Scottish Border.

Kendal, the largest town in the old county of Westmorland, has always been a bustling place, from the days when it was on the main route to Scotland. Nowadays the M6 and the Kendal by-pass divert much of the traffic away from the town centre, but its narrow main streets, Highgate, Stramongate and Stricklandgate, are still busy, and the fine stage-coaching inns of the 17th and 18th century, to which Bonnie Prince Charlie is said to have retreated after his abortive 1745 rebellion, still line these streets.

The Castle Inn, Kendal

Close to the castle in Kendal, tucked away just off the A685 is the friendly little **CASTLE INN.** Run by Des and Babs for the past ten years it has a very friendly atmosphere and is an ideal family pub. It has a bright exterior with lovely hanging baskets, and inside, beamed ceilings and lots of ornamental brass. Food is served every day between 12 - 2.00pm in the lounge bar or there are tables outside; the games room makes an interesting diversion. There is a wide range of ales on sale with guest beers changed each week. The Inn has bed and breakfast accommodation in two letting rooms and is good value.

The Castle Inn, Castle Street, Kendal, Cumbria. Tel: 01539 729983

Another distinctive feature of the historic centre is the series of named or numbered 'yards', tucked away down alleyways and through arches, once the focus of local small industry. Walking down Highgate their intriguing, narrow entrances are irresistible to anyone with a sense of curiosity.

Stricklandgate runs past the **TOWN HALL**, which still houses Katherine Parr's Book of Devotions, and turns into Highgate.

While you're on Highgate, look into the **BREWERY ARTS CENTRE**, which combines a theatre, with an excellent programme of touring productions, an art gallery, cinema and a cafe.

At the bottom of Highgate is the **ABBOT HALL MUSEUM OF LAKELAND LIFE AND INDUSTRY**, themed around traditional rural trades of the region, such as blacksmiths' or wheelwrights' workshops, agricultural activity, weaving and printing. There are re-created cottage interiors and elegantly furnished period rooms. Abbot Hall Art Gallery forms part of a complex within **ABBOT HALL PARK** and includes work by John Ruskin and the celebrated Kendal painter, George Romney.

Adjacent to Abbot Hall is the 13th century **PARISH CHURCH OF KENDAL**, one of the largest in England with five aisles and a peel of ten bells.

The Parish Church, Kendal

Close to the centre of Kendal on Windermere Road is the **HILLCREST PRIVATE HOTEL**, a Victorian house built of lakeland limestone, it is situated on the main road which runs from Kendal through the Lake District and makes for easy access to all Lakeland areas. The bedrooms have en-suite bathrooms and there is a comfortable lounge in which to relax. The proprietor has provided bed and breakfast accommodation here for eighteen years and will ensure you have a comfortable and happy stay. The hotel is open all year round and there is a private car park.

The Hillcrest Private Hotel, 98 Windermere Road, Kendal, Cumbria.
Tel: 01539 722680

Kendal is a good centre from which to explore South Cumbria. There is good railway and motorway access and some surprisingly nice walks from the town, along the River Kent or into the surrounding limestone hills. It is this stone that gives the buildings the distinctive, pale grey colour which is such a familiar characteristic of the Lake District.

Around Kendal

If you leave Kendal heading towards the nearby village of Burneside **THE SAWYERS ARMS** on Burneside Road is just five minutes walk from the town centre.

The Sawyers Arms

This popular pub is run by Barbara and Geoff Wilson who came here six years ago and have completely renovated the place. Originally two houses, it became a pub in the late 19th century and still maintains old-fashioned, traditional values. It is immediately apparent that this is a place where people of all ages get together for a chat as they have done for the past 100 years. The piano in the corner proves a big attraction, with good old-fashioned knees-ups and singalongs of an evening and the live music on Saturday evenings is very popular. The pub is open all day every day and lunchtime bar snacks are available, which on a fine day can be enjoyed in the pretty beer garden at the rear. Barbara and Geoff also offer bed and breakfast accommodation in seven pleasant and airy rooms so you can enjoy this friendly atmosphere for longer.

The Sawyers Arms, Stricklandgate, Kendal Tel: 01539 729737

WEBBS GARDEN CENTRE has a 3 acre site with a vast selection of plants, shrubs, trees, and more besides. Originally set up in 1810 by a nurseryman called James Meldrum, the business was bought from him in the mid 1800's by Clarence Webb and has stayed in the Webb family to this day. It was Clarence who back in the late 1800's introduced the now internationally acclaimed Webbs Wonderful lettuce renowned for its crisp heart, and in 1922 James Webb developed a growing area for what became his award-winning varieties of dahlias and chrysanthemums. Later, James' son Geoffrey took over the business and moved it to its present site on Burneside Road where it is now a thriving business run by Geoffrey's daughter Judith and her husband Bill Stocker.

Webbs Garden Centre

Open 7 days a week, Webbs Garden Centre has a friendly atmosphere and a knowledgeable and helpful team of staff to ensure you get whatever you need. The layout of the centre also makes it easily accessible for the disabled. The house plant section is a delight, with a rich variety of both common and lesser known plants, whilst outside you will find an extensive conifer rearing area, and rows of rhododendrons, rose bushes, raspberry canes and fruit trees.

Back inside the main building you can't miss the vast array of awards which virtually cover one wall, an indication of Webbs Garden Centre's successes over the past 100 years. The centre's recent extension houses a selection of quality garden furniture and barbecue equipment. Whilst in the lovely pine panelled restaurant you can relax and enjoy a tasty home-made snack. As you prepare to leave, you will doubtless be drawn to the gift shop which is full of tempting items which make perfect mementoes of a lovely day out, and from October to December there is the added attraction of an extensive Christmas display.

Webbs Garden Centre, Burneside Road, Kendal, Cumbria.
Tel: 01539 720068

Continuing along the A685 the scenery changes quite suddenly to open fields and hillsides, and eventually the road comes to the village of Grayrigg.

GRAYRIGG, is a fine village where a cluster of alms houses, cottages and a simple church form a lovely rural setting. This was the birthplace of Francis Howgill, 1610-69, who introduced George Fox to the Westmorland 'Seekers', a group of radical Christians from the area. Their meeting led directly to the establishment of the Quaker Church, the Society of Friends.

HYNING COTTAGES may not be the easiest to find, but are ideal for *The Hidden Places*; - the end reward being well worth the seeking. Fortunately, Allen & Myra Marshall, the resident owners of these charming self-catering cottages can supply all the directional information in detail.

Hyning Cottages

Sheltering in a secluded valley offering peace and tranquillity, the cottages are only 500 yards off the A685, four miles from the M6. and the shops of Kendal are only a few miles away. 'Hyning' is a 350 year old farmhouse where visitors are welcomed to the four holiday cottages which have been carefully converted from the adjoining barns. All the properties have a very high standard of furnishings and fittings, Economy 7 electric heating, Colour television and bed linen is also included.

The modern kitchens have a conventional oven and a microwave oven. The cottages have a wealth of old oak beams and are full of character. Many rooms have splendid views of the countryside and surrounding fells. There are plenty of facilities including laundry, payphone and ample parking. Children under six and the family pet can accommodated by prior arrangement. Allen and Myra carried out substantial conversions to the property over a period of four years and clearly created delightful holiday accommodation set in wonderful surroundings. Four Keys Commended by Tourist Board. The extra good news is: - Open all year!

Hyning Cottages, Hyning, Nr. Grayrigg, Kendal, Cumbria.
Tel: 01539 824627

PATTON, near to Grayrigg is a peaceful the little rural village located only four miles from Kendal.

The award winning **FIELD END BARNS** in Patton are tastefully converted farm buildings (with ETB four key classification) which form five excellent holiday homes, set in 200 acres of farm and woodland. These spacious and well-equipped houses are ideal for family or group holidays and their location makes them particularly safe for small children with the nearest road being 1/3 mile away. There are many beautiful walks literally on the doorstep and fishing and horse riding are available within a mile. A mobile shop calls once a week providing most essentials and the milkman delivers three times a week. For a holiday at your own pace in idyllic surroundings, Field End Barns is ideal.

The owners have recently restored **SHAW END MANSION** and converted it to provide four most luxurious apartments providing surroundings on the scale of a stately home. The two hundred acre estate is situated four miles north east of Kendal and must surely offer one of the most prestigious locations in the area.

Field End Barns, Field End, Patton, Cumbria. Tel: 01539 824220

BURNESIDE is a couple of miles along this road from Kendal. There have been settlements here since the Stone Age, as is reflected by the remains of a stone circle on **POTTER FELL**.

By the 15th century Burneside was a settled agricultural area. A rich variety of mills sprang up along the River Sprint - fulling, corn, cotton, wool, bobbin and the original rag paper mill at Cowan Head.

If you have been in the Lake District for any length time you will probably have come across **ENGLISH LAKES ICE CREAM**. This small, family run dairy, makes and supplies ice creams to businesses all over Cumbria and was voted in the top six in the UK for superb quality. Using fresh farm milk and cream the Lawson family produce a full range of real fruit ice creams and sorbets and special diabetic ice cream. Visitors are welcome to look round the factory and watch production; there is also the opportunity to purchase the produce from the small shop. Situated 3 miles from Kendal, 8 miles from Windermere and with beautiful riverside walks close by this makes an interesting and refreshing visit.

Winstanley Dairy, Bowston, Near Burneside Tel: 01539 730183

BRIGSTEER. A right turn off the main Milnthorpe Road will bring you to this little hamlet, about three miles away from Kendal, between the parishes of Levens and Helsington. Snugly settled under the limestone escarpment of **SCOUT SCAR**, Brigsteer is a very pretty village right off the beaten track.

From the middle of Brigsteer follow the road which leads into **BRIGSTEER WOOD**. The climate is milder here than Helsington and other nearby villages, perhaps because of its sheltered position, shown by the fine early flowering gardens and the prolific daffodils, early orchids, lily of the valley and other wild flowers in the Wood.

LEVENS is on the southern tip of Scout Scar, overlooking the Lyth Valley and the lower reaches of the River Kent. Here you must see **LEVENS HALL** and its unique Topiary Garden.

The Elizabethan mansion developed from a 13th century pele tower and the garden was laid out in 1692. Levens Hall is said to be haunted by three ghosts, a black dog, a lady in pink and a gypsy woman who, legend has it, put a curse on the family saying that they would have no heir until the River Kent ceased to flow and a white fawn was born in the Park. In fact after many years without a direct heir, in 1895 the River Kent froze over and a white fawn was born too, and a son and heir was born.

Levens Hall

SIZERGH, the neighbouring village, has its share of similar tales. At **SIZERGH CASTLE**, an impressive National Trust estate, the ghost of the Lady of the Castle in medieval times is said to haunt the Castle screaming to be released from the room that her fiercely jealous husband locked her in and where she starved to death while he was away in battle.

The Strickland Arms

THE STRICKLAND ARMS, a traditional Victorian inn on the doorstep of Sizergh Castle, is also owned by the National Trust. It is a charming building overlooking a large, well-kept beer garden. Inside the atmosphere is warm and welcoming, with a good selection of fine ales and excellent food. Alistair and Kirsten who run the inn provide a variety of freshly prepared bar snacks daily, with an a'la carte restaurant both providing excellent value for money. whilst the restaurant itself is reminiscent of a grand drawing room, being cosy, intimate and welcoming.

Once a month Alistair and Kirsten have a "themed" evening, with appropriate food and atmosphere supplied. Ranging from Italian, Spanish

Sizergh Castle

and other foreign evenings, to the occasional Country and Western night, these make a popular attraction of this charming inn. Bed and Breakfast Accommodation is available with the evening meal an option upon request. All rooms are 'doubles' with shared facilities and have views overlooking the Cumbrian Fells.

The Strickland Arms, Sizergh, Nr. Kendal. Tel: 01539 560239

From the main gate to Sizergh Castle, you will see a sign to the **BARN SHOP AND TEAROOM.** These are fairly recent additions to **LOW SIZERGH FARM,** a working dairy farm which stands in 275 acres of lovely Cumbrian countryside. Set within a 17th century Westmorland stone barn, the farm shop on the ground floor offers a wide selection of superb farm made cheeses, Jersey ice cream, fresh vegetables (some organic), preserves, pickles, hampers and free-range/organic turkeys (when in season)

Upstairs in the gallery an abundance of dried flowers, hops, gifts, crafts and cards of every description can be found. To complete your visit, pause a while in the charming rustic tearoom which overlooks the milking parlour, and sample the home-made light lunches, mouthwatering freshly baked farmhouse cakes, pies, scones and cream teas whilst you watch the cows being milked.

Barn Shop and Tearoom, Low Sizergh Farm, Near Kendal Tel: 01539 560426

A pleasant journey towards Kirkby Lonsdale can be made from here by taking the back lanes passing quiet villages such as Sedgwick and Stainton, until you join the A65 at its junction with the M6.

Just a short a distance of three miles from Kendal, along the A65 (Kendal to M6 Junc.36) take the turn to **OXENHOLME** Railway Station, just up the hill on the right hand side is a small, friendly, family run guest house known as **THE GLEN.** This is an ideal centre for touring the Lake District and Yorkshire Dales. There are three spacious letting bedrooms with en-suite bathrooms, tea and coffee making facilities, colour television and with views of the fells. A full four course evening meal can be booked from a comprehensive menu with vegetarian meals on request.

Children over the age of 12 years can be accommodated. Good private car parking space. Please respect the 'no smoking' policy.

The Glen, Oxenholme, Kendal, Cumbria.   Tel: 01539 726386

Travel out from Kendal along the A6 for six miles and shortly after passing the Plough Inn at **SELSIDE**, take the next left turn to arrive at **LOW JOCK SCAR,** a small country guest house in a charming setting. The house is located in a wonderfully secluded riverside setting surrounded by six acres of garden and woodland and excellent walking can be enjoyed nearby,   There are five double/twin bedrooms (three en-suite) with good views of the garden, two of which are on the ground floor. All rooms have tea and coffee making facilities. Guests have their own comfortable lounge with television which is well stocked with maps and books for walkers and motorists. Dinner can be provided by arrangement where fresh produce and home cooking are combined. There is a no smoking policy in the house. You will find a relaxed, friendly and helpful atmosphere here. Closed Nov. to early March.

Low Jock Scar, Selside, Kendal, Cumbria.   Tel: 01539 823259

CROOKLANDS. Situated near Crooklands, halfway between Kendal and Kirkby Lonsdale is **PRESTON PATRICK HALL**, a medieval Manor House, now the farmhouse of a 500 acre beef and sheep farm.

It was built in the late 14th century and has a 'Great Hall' and 'Court Room' which has a magnificent 15th century timbered roof - and is open to the public by appointment. **PRESTON PATRICK HALL COTTAGE** is a self-contained wing of the Manor House. It offers self-catering accommodation for two or three people, plus the option of an extra bedroom sleeping another three. It has thick stone walls, exposed beams, antique furniture and double glazing throughout. All modern amenities are included and lovely views can be enjoyed from the main rooms. Guests are allowed limited use of the heated, enclosed swimming pool and there is table tennis, farm walks and beck fishing to be enjoyed. No pets please and Wellingtons might be useful in the farm area.

Preston Patrick Hall Cottage, Preston Patrick Hall, Crooklands, Milnthorpe, Cumbria. Tel. & Fax - 015395 67200

On the B6254 Carnforth road, midway between WHITTINGTON and ARKHOLME, you will find **NEWTON HOLME FARM**, home of **TOBILANE DESIGNS**, a super toy workshop where you can see traditional toys manufactured in the time-honoured way.

Newton Holme Farm, home of Tobilane Designs

Each item is beautifully handcrafted, from the brightly coloured wooden mobiles and intriguing Jacob's Ladder, to the wonderful ride-on

Thomas the Tank Engine and woolly rocking sheep - after all why should horses have all the fun! This really is a treasure trove of delight and the only difficulty with your visit here is how to get everyone to leave - and we don't just mean the children!

Tobilane Designs, Newton Holme Farm, Nr Carnforth, Lancs.
Tel: 015242 72662

KIRKBY LONSDALE, the old town on the banks of the River Lune (hence its name), is almost on the edge of the Yorkshire Dales National Park. Despite the conflict of allegiances, this town has maintained its character over the years, and as it is set well back from the main A65 road, it remains a very traditional, handsome market town, where life still revolves around the market place and its 600 year old cross.

Lovely Georgian buildings crowd along the winding main street and there are interesting alleyways and courtyards to explore with good shops to browse in, delicious bakeries and some wonderful tea shops.

The **SNOOTY FOX TAVERN** is a listed Jacobean Inn in the centre of Kirkby Lonsdale and for a long time has had a reputation for good wholesome cooking, efficient friendly service and fine cask ales. Under the guiding hand of proprietor Jack Shone, his young and enthusiastic team set amazing standards; in this Westmorland Market Town they average over one hundred meals a day - all year round.

The Snooty Fox Tavern

With a team of six professionals in the kitchen, the chefs, led by Gordon Cartwright, are very serious about what they do for a living. Gordon is a member of the institute of The Master Chefs of Great Britain and was proclaimed by the Daily Telegraph as one of Britain's top chefs. He is responsible for the daily preparation of over forty freshly cooked dishes including Soufflés, Lobster, Homemade bread, home crafted desserts and original chocolates. The newly refurbished accommodation at the 'Snooty' boasts nine en-suite rooms all with luxury facilities, attractive drapes and antique furnishings. A breakfast buffet is provided in the restaurant where both continental and full English Breakfast is

17

served. The two traditional bars serve hand pumped ales and the bar menu covers all levels of requirements while maintaining the quality. You are guaranteed culinary choice at this establishment.

Snooty Fox Tavern, Kirkby Lonsdale, Cumbria.
Tel: 015242 71308 Fax: 015242 72642

The view from the churchyard is delightful, extending over the valley of the Lune to the fells beyond. J.M.W. Turner was inspired to paint this very scene and John Ruskin wrote enthusiastically to write about what he saw - *"The Valley of the Lune at Kirkby Lonsdale is one of the loveliest scenes in England..."*. Since then, the name Ruskin's View has stuck.

The arched bridge over the River Lune below the town, **DEVIL'S BRIDGE**, is reputed to be at least 600 years old, and got its name from the legend of an old woman who, unable to cross the deep river with her cattle, asked the devil to build her a bridge. He duly did this in return for the soul of the first creature to cross. But the clever woman threw a stick across the bridge which was collected by her dog, cheating the devil of a human soul, and he disappears with a howl of rage, leaving behind his neck collar which some say can still be seen in the river below. Today on summer Sundays leather-clad bikers use the bridge as an informal gathering place and an impressive display of motorbikes from every era can be admired.

The drive from Kirkby Lonsdale to Sedbergh, on the A683 which follows the River Lune upstream, is quite beautiful. The river forms the geographic western boundary of the Yorkshire Dales National Park, a gentle valley on the edge of fertile farmland and rolling hills.

Garghyll Dyke

GARGHYLL DYKE is a traditional working dairy farm offering bed and breakfast accommodation three miles from Kirby Lonsdale off the A65 at Cowan Bridge. Some of the farmhouse buildings date back to 1850 and it has been a family run farm for four generations - guests are welcome to explore. The bedrooms are tastefully furnished each with

Devil's Bridge, Kirkby Lonsdale

washbasin and tea and coffee facilities. Country pubs nearby offer plenty of variety for evening meals and you will be served a hearty breakfast to start your day. Pets accommodated by arrangement. Reductions for children. Open March - October. Tourist Board One Crown Highly Commended.

Garghyll Dyke, Cowan Bridge, Kirby Lonsdale, Cumbria. Tel: 015242 71446

CASTERTON is reached after a short drive from Kirkby Lonsdale. A pretty village of grey stone cottages and a church with a remarkable collection of Victorian paintings by Henry Holiday and James Clark, the village is perhaps best known for its Girls Boarding School which has links with the Brontes.

On the main road between Sedbergh and Dent, not far from the M6 motorway, is the **DENT CRAFTS CENTRE**. Owned by Matty Bradley, the centre is housed in a converted hay barn which was once a print workshop and an old and working Victorian printing press remains from that time. There are several resident craftsmen and women on the premises who happily demonstrate their skills to interested onlookers. There is a picture gallery, with original oils, watercolours and etchings by local artists, small country antiques and primitive folk art, pottery, candles, metal work and much more to enjoy. The centre restaurant and coffee shop, Scoffers, specialises in home baking and is open daily for coffee, teas and light meals. Dinner, on Friday, Saturday and Sunday evenings, can be taken in the delightful candle lit restaurant. Booking is essential as the restaurant's excellent reputation has spread far and wide and is also recommended by Egon Ronay.

Finally, bed and breakfast and self-catering accommodation is available in another beautifully converted spacious and relaxing barn. The crafts centre is a must for anyone interested in the skills of yesterday and in viewing a range of high quality unusual and traditionally made products.

Dent Crafts Centre, Helmside, Dent Tel: 015396 25400

The views on the A65 to Sedburgh are spectacular, but it is worth taking some of the side roads on the way to explore some of the villages and walks right on the Yorkshire Dales border.

Leave the main road at the little village of **BARBON**, shortly after Casterton, and travel up Barbondale and past the wooded estate of Barbon Park into Dentdale, to Dent, in one of Cumbria's finest vales.

DENT has a delightful cobbled main street with tall cottages where the famous *terrible knitters* of Dent produced stockings and gloves for sale at Kendal Market. A fountain of pinkish Shap granite in the village centre indicates Dent's links with Professor Adam Sedgwick, 1785-1853. Wood-wardian Professor of Geology at Cambridge University, Sedgwick was one of the greatest field geologists of all time. He never forgot his native dale and wrote a moving account of the valley as it had been in his childhood.

The Sedgwick Fountain, Dent

The little valley winds past old farms and hamlets to **LEA YEAT** where a steep lane hairpins up to **DENT RAILWAY STATION**, almost five miles outside Dent. This is a marvellous place to begin a ramble into Dentdale or over the Whernside. Dent is the highest railway station in Britain, over 1100 ft above sea level, and is on the route of the famous Settle-Carlisle Railway line.

GARSDALE, just north of Dentdale, is both a dale and a village, overlooked by the dramatic Baugh Fell. The Clough River follows the dale from Garsdale Head, the watershed into Wensleydale, where a row of Midland Railway cottages lies alongside the former junction station on the Settle-Carlisle line. This is now a surprisingly busy little place during the summer months, where preserved steam locomotives pause to take water from a moorland spring.

SEDBERGH is a town of subtle character, set in countryside of outstanding beauty. An old market town with cobbled streets, it is dwarfed by some of Alfred Wainwright's favourite fells, the mighty Howgills, Firbank Fells and Baugh Fell.

It is Sedburgh's location in the midst of this striking scenery that has made it such a thriving community for hundreds of years, at the confluence of four valleys and four rivers where ancient trade routes merged. The market dates back as far as the 13th century.

Please Don't Forget...

To tell people that you read about them in

The Hidden Places

One mile outside Sedbergh on the A684 is **FARFIELD COUNTRY GUEST HOUSE.** Set in two acres of gardens, it was originally built in the 1840's for a local mill owner. Now run by Mike and Liz Clark, it has seven well equipped and tastefully furnished bedrooms, some en-suite, all with tea and coffee making facilities and outstanding views. There is an attractive dinning room and two lounges, one with a log fire for chillier evenings. In addition there are three self-catering units available. One is a lovely well-furnished bungalow attached to the main house which sleeps two, the other two are static vans, one sleeping 2-4 people and the other 4-8 people, all connected to mains and both with en-suite facilities. Group bookings are welcome, guided walks are available on request. Evening meals are available as are packed lunches on request.

Farfield Country House, Hawes Road, Sedbergh, Cumbria.
Tel: 015396 20537

This area is filled with Quaker history. In the Firbank Fells, Firbank Knott can be said to be the birthplace of Quakerism for it was here, in 1652, that the visionary George Fox gave his great sermon to inspire over a thousand 'seekers' from the whole of the North of England. This was to lead to the development of the Quaker movement.

If you take the little lane which runs along the back of Firbank Fell , about half a mile west of the B6357, you can walk up to **FOX'S PULPIT**, a simple boulder marked with a plaque just a short way from the roadside, where George Fox delivered his momentous words.

BRIGFLATTS is just off the A683 to the south of Sedburgh and a lovely riverside and field walk from the town. Here, close to where Fox stayed overnight with his friend Richard Robinson, is one of the oldest Quaker meeting houses in the world, a beautiful, simple building where Friends met for communal worship.

THE HOWGILL FELLS, a series of magnificent, open hills, most of them ancient common-land, provide some of the most spectacular countryside in the North of England for the dedicated hill-walker.

Several tracks and old green-ways lead across them but you can also wander over the open summits, making your way to such peaks as **ULDALE HEAD**, **YARLSIDE** and **THE CALF**, at 2219 ft the highest point in the Howgills. The most spectacular feature of the Howgills is **CAUTLEY CRAG**, a great cliff several hundred feet high, alongside which a beautiful narrow waterfall, **CAUTLEY SPOUT**, tumbles.

Experienced walkers can reach the waterfall from The Calf but for most people it is more easily reached from the footpath that leads from **THE CROSS KEYS**, a 17th century inn which is now a temperance hotel. Here is a place for the real lover of good food and a wonderful surprise for people who have never been before. It is owned by The National Trust, tiny and very old, not sophisticated, but comfortable and homely and full of character. There are log fires and plenty of books, but no television or smoking anywhere. Guests bring their own drinks and glasses are supplied. Evening meals may be booked by non-residents at 24 hours notice.

The Cross Keys Hotel, Cautley, Sedbergh 01539 620284

CAUTLEY is on the A683, about three miles outside Sedbergh towards Kirkby Stephen, another stunning stretch of road to drive along in the Rawthey Valley. The road follows the River Rauthey and is one of those beautiful routes through the high fells that only a few people find.

For campers and walkers this area is a perfect place to be based for a holiday, surrounded on all sides by the best English walking country, with the Lake District and the Yorkshire Dales National Parks to choose from.

CHAPTER TWO

The Upper Eden Valley

Crosby Garrett

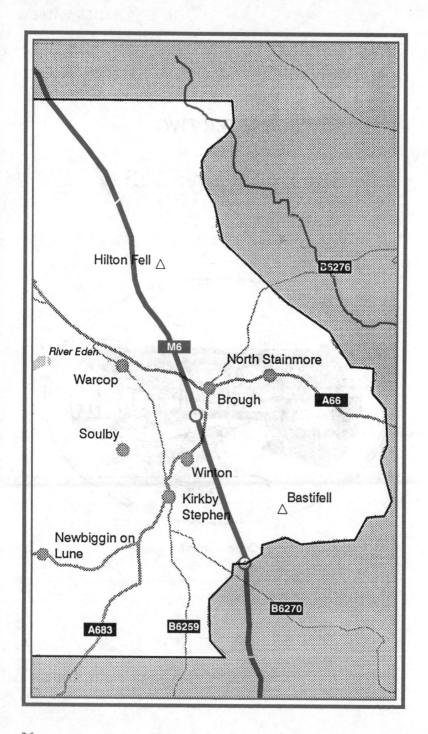

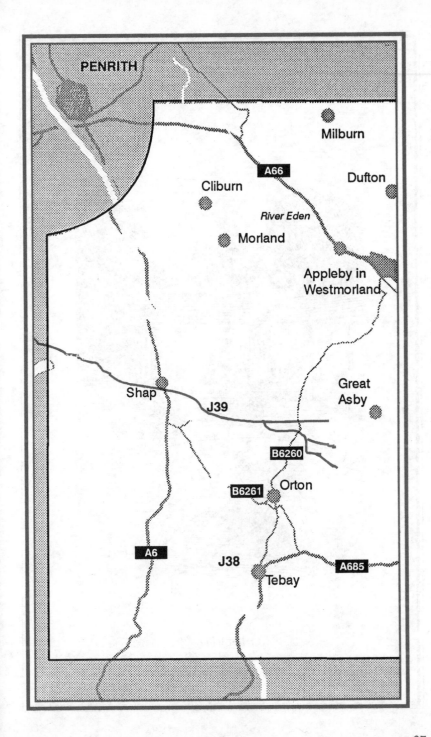

Orton Village

CHAPTER TWO

• The Upper Eden Valley

THE RIVER EDEN is entirely Cumbrian and one of the few large rivers in England that flows northwards. It rises on the edge of the Yorkshire Dales, in the fells above Mallerstang, and ends its journey in the Solway Firth. Carved through boulder clay and red sandstone and sandwiched between the Lakeland Fells and the Northern Pennines, the Eden Valley is green and fertile - in every sense another 'Eden'.

The valley was vulnerable to Scottish raids in medieval times and the number of pele towers and castles in the area are testament to a turbulent and often violent past.

The Eden shares its course with the famous Settle-Carlisle railway line, whose highest point is at Aisgill (1169 ft). Here it is joined by the infant river before descending through the steeply sided valley of Mallerstang. This is a particularly remote and beautiful area; to the west is **WILD BOAR FELL**, a great brooding, flat-topped peak where reputedly the last wild boar in England was killed. Tucked down in the valley are the romantic ruins of Pendragon and **LAMMERSIDE CASTLE**. Lammerside originally dates from the 12th century but only the remains of the keep survive.

PENDRAGON CASTLE is shrouded in legend which claims it to be the castle of Uther Pendragon, father of King Arthur, in the 6th century. Its name suggests that the castle was built by Uther, but at that time it would have been made of wood. It was some time after 1092 that William Rufus, having conquered Carlisle, built a stone pele tower at Pendragon to guard the pass of Mallerstang. In 1268 the castle passed into the hands of the Clifford family. Twice it was burned by the Scots and repaired by the family, the second time, in 1660, by the most famous member of that family, Lady Anne Clifford.

Between **GARSDALE HEAD** and Kirkby Stephen, the B6259 follows the dramatic course of this valley, along with the Eden and the Settle-Carlisle railway line. Three miles from Garsdale Head, you will come to the remote hamlet of MALLERSTANG

OUTGHILL is about a mile north of Pendragon Castle. Here, St Mary's Church, first built in 1311, was also repaired by Lady Anne. Indeed, from 1643, when she finally got possession of the Clifford estates, 38 years after her father's death, until 1675 she devoted her life to restoring her properties and living in each of them for varying periods of time. The estates included six castles, Skipton and Barden in West Yorkshire and Appleby, Brough, Brougham and Pendragon in Westmorland. She even repaired the ancient Roman road between Wensleydale and the Eden Valley, the route she so often took to travel between her beloved Eden Valley castles and her birthplace, Skipton. Locals called it **LADY ANNE'S WAY**. It is also aptly called the High Way, as it was 'worked' for many years by highwaymen, and none more notorious than Dick Turpin and William 'Swift Nick' Nevison.

Beyond Pendragon a narrow lane swings westward off the A683 Sedburgh to Kirkby Stephen Road, over the shoulder of Wild Boar Fell to RAVENSTONEDALE (or Rissendale, as it is known locally), passing through some superb limestone scenery with great rock outcrops and the crumbling remains of once flourishing lime-kilns. Ravenstonedale lies on the very edge of the Howgill Fells and is a pretty, fellside village of stone-built cottages around Scandal Beck.

THE PARISH CHURCH OF ST. OSWALD is especially interesting. Built in 1738, it is one of the few Georgian churches in Cumbria. An earlier church had a separate bell-tower which rested on pillars and at its centre hung a refuge bell. Anyone guilty of a capital offence who managed to escape to Ravenstonedale and sound the bell was free from arrest by the King's officials. This custom was finally abolished in the reign of James I.

The present church, surrounded by yew trees, is particularly unusual with its bow pews facing one another and its three-decker pulpit complete with a sounding board and a seat for the parson's wife. The window at the east end commemorates the last woman in England to be put to death for her protestant faith. Elizabeth Gaunt was sentenced in 1638 by the notorious Judge Jeffries to be burnt at the stake for sheltering a fugitive rebel.

KIRKBY STEPHEN is where the Eden Valley widens into a fertile plain of red sandstone villages, well tended farms and small market towns. Kirkby Stephen is old, very old! It was the Norsemen who first established a village here and the Vikings named it, 'Kirke and bye', meaning churchtown. Although essentially part of the Eden Valley, Kirkby Stephen has a strong Yorkshire Dales feel about it. Indeed, the **CHURCH OF ST. STEPHEN'S**, with its long, elegant nave, has been called "the cathedral of the Dales".

The church dates from 1220, with a 16th century tower, and is one of the finest churches in the Eastern fells, dominating the northern end of the town from its elevated position.

Until the last century **THE TRUPP STONE** in the churchyard received money from local people every Easter Monday in payment of church tithes. At eight o'clock the curfew is still sounded by **THE TAGGY BELL**, once regarded by local children as a demon.

Inside the church are a number of pre-Conquest stones, some of which show Norse influence. The most remarkable is the 8th century **LOKI STONE**, of which there are only two in Europe. Loki was a Norse God and presumably Viking settlers brought the belief in Loki to Kirkby Stephen. The carving of Loki shows a figure resembling the devil with sheep's horns, whose legs and arms are bound by heavy irons. This image is symbolic of the overpowering of Paganism by Christian beliefs. For many years the stone lay undiscovered, re-used as a building stone.

The tomb of Sir Richard De Musgrave of Harcla Castle is also in this church. He was the man reputed to have killed that last wild boar upon Wild Boar Fell, and the story was given credence when some years ago the tomb was opened to reveal the bones of a man and woman alongside two tusks from a boar.

The Kings Arms Hotel

The attractive **KINGS ARMS HOTEL** lies in the main street of the historic market town Kirkby Stephen. Dating back to the 17th century, this former posting and coaching inn has also acted as a tax collection office. Many of the building's original features remain including the Powder Closet on the landing. The hotel offers excellent accommodation in nine first class bedrooms which, though modern in their facilities and comfort, retain the character of the old building. Personally run by John and his friendly staff you are in good hands and will be sure to enjoy your stay.

All the delicious, home-cooked meals are served in the attractive dining room that is furnished with antiques and decorated with fine tapestries and the intimate cocktail bar is the perfect place for a pre-dinner drink. Open to non-residents as well, the Kings Arms Hotel is a popular inn with locals and visitors alike.

Kings Arms Hotel, Kirkby Stephen Tel: 017683 71378

Between the church and the market-place stand **THE CLOISTERS** which served for a long time as a butter market. The market itself has existed since 1351 and has always been a focus for the surrounding countryside, whose industry was largely agricultural. In the 18th century knitting - mostly of stockings - was the most important manufacture of the town, and a restored spinning gallery reflects the importance of the woollen industry.

There are many delightful walks from Kirkby Stephen, for example to **CROGLAM EARTHWORKS**, a pre-historic fort, or to nearby **STENKRITH PARK**. There are also some pleasant strolls along the riverside to a fine waterfall where the River Eden cascades into **COOP KARNEL HOLE**. Look out for the unusual shapes of the weathered limestone rock.

Kirkby Stephen

If you like the 'away from it all' style of holiday, you could book a static caravan with Nick and Rosemary Paul at **SAWBRIDGE HALL** off the B6260 midway between Appleby and Kirkby Stephen. The three vans are well sited on a gently sloping area of grassland fenced and enclosed by trees. It's easy to while away the hours here in such peaceful countryside; ideal for walking and bird watching and a good place for pets which must be controllable when in the area of farm animals. Sawbridge Hall is also a working dairy and sheep farm, and visitors, especially children, are encouraged to join in and help (wellies needed). The vans provide good, clean accommodation and basic amenities enabling families to take an easy-going holiday.

Sawbridge Hall, Self-catering static caravans, Bleatarn, Appleby, Cumbria.
Tel: 017683 41201

NATEBY, close to Kirkby Stephen, is well worth visiting. The road follows the old corpse-route over **COFFIN BRIDGE**, along which the dead were taken to Kirkby Stephen to be buried.

The village is now a quiet hamlet of houses standing alongside a beck. For centuries previously it was dominated by Hartley Castle, probably built in the 13th century and the home of Sir Andrew De Harcala, a great soldier during the reign of Edward II. Harcala was one of the first men to fight on a pony and he was made Earl of Carlisle in recognition of his service to the Crown. However, his failure to prevent Robert the Bruce invading the North of England led him to be accused of treason and he was executed in 1325. His castle was finally demolished by the Musgrave family who used the stone to build their Manor House at Edenhall.

Above Hartley you can still see the early **BELLPITS** in which copper and lead were mined and there is a fine walk from the village up to **NINE STANDARDS RIGG**, one of the Eden Valley's most imposing landmarks. The cairns mark the old boundary between Yorkshire and Westmorland. According to legend they were first erected to represent the flags, or standards, of a great English army camped between the passes of Stainmore and Mallerstang.

TEBAY, to the west of Kirkby Stephen, is on the A685 road to Kendal. The road follows the course of the upper reaches of the River Lune. At one time a sheep-farming area and railway village, Tebay, a long rambling village, now owes its importance to the arrival of the M6 motorway, Cumbria's main thoroughfare. While this may not be a particularly attractive asset, its very central and easily accessible location makes this a very convenient base for touring Cumbria, and the surrounding scenery is just as beautiful.

THE CROSS KEYS is a famous old coaching inn standing at Tebay on the A685 Kendal to Brough road. Dating back some 400 years, the Cross Keys lies at the bottom of the difficult and arduous assent to Shap Summit. The village grew up around the railway and the London to Scotland line can be seen from here as can the M6 motorway.

The Cross Keys

A charming inn, owned and personally run by Jackie and Peter

Baister, the Cross Keys is full of character and charm. With very low beams, this is a warm and friendly inn that serves excellent beer and delicious food. With six spacious guest bedrooms it is also a super place to stay.

The Cross Keys, Tebay Tel: 015396 24240

WINTON, a quiet and picturesque hamlet, is about a mile to the north of Kirkby Stephen towards Brough and can be reached by turning east off the A685.

Winton, in old English, means "pasture farmland". It is built on a spring-line and like many other Cumbrian villages of medieval origin, once followed the *runrig*, or two-field system of agriculture. You can still find the evidence in long, thin fields to the north of the village. These would have been individual strips in medieval, open fields which were enclosed in the 17th and 18th centuries.

In the centre of the village is **THE MANOR HOUSE**, built in 1726, Winton's only three-storey building. It was formerly a boys' school where apparently the boys were treated like prisoners and not allowed to return home until the end of their education in case they told of their life at the school,

The oldest building is **WINTON HALL**, built of stone and dated 1665, but its appearance suggests it to be older with its stone buttresses and mullioned windows with iron bars.

The **BAY HORSE INN**, in a splendid position overlooking Winton's village, is an impressive pub, eating place and bed and breakfast establishment which is well worth making a detour to visit. Originally constructed between 1620 and 1630 as a farmhouse, the building became an alehouse late in the 17th century and then an inn early in the 18th century. At one time, part of the building was used to keep a horse and dray which belonged to a local Kirkby Stephen brewer.

The Bay Horse Inn

The present day inn still retains much of its original character and charm with attractive white-painted walls and a cosy traditional interior.

It has been owned and personally run since 1985 by Sheila and Derek Parvin, two fine hosts who have been successful in creating a truly relaxed and welcoming atmosphere. The inn is a freehouse and during the summer months, stocks as many as five traditional hand-pulled ales, all well kept and served in top-class condition. An extensive menu of delicious bar meals is also served every lunchtime and evening. All dishes are home-made and come in generous portions at surprisingly reasonable prices. Sheila and Derek have also created three tastefully decorated letting bedrooms which are available all year round. These all have central heating, en-suite facilities and are appointed to a good modern standard. In fine weather, customers are welcome to sit out in the attractive garden which is situated to the rear of the inn. All in all, the Bay Horse Inn offers excellent food, drink and hospitality.

Bay Horse Inn, Winton, Near Kirkby Stephen Tel: 01768 371451

Walking on **WINTON FELL** you are more than likely to see red grouse lifting off from the large tracts of heather on the fellside. Indeed the wildlife is much more prolific around this area where the limestone provides more plentiful food than on the fells around the lakes.

KABER is a few miles from Winton and, in 1663, was the scene of the Kaber Rigg plot, a rebellion against Charles II. It was led by Captain Robert Atkinson of Watergate Farm in Mallerstang. The rising failed and Atkinson was hung, drawn and quartered at Appleby; tragically, a messenger carrying his reprieve was delayed on Stainmore.

BROUGH is a small town which stands at the point where the Stainmore Pass opens into the Vale of Eden. It is, in effect, two settlements - Church Brough and Market Brough.

CHURCH BROUGH is a group of neat houses and cottages clustered around a little market square in which a maypole stands on the site of a former market-cross.

BROUGH CASTLE is built within the ramparts of the Roman camp of Verterae, constructed to protect the Roman road over Stainmore Pass. The building of the Norman castle was begun by William Rufus in 1095 but it was largely destroyed in 1174 by William the Lion of Scotland. Many times Scottish raiders laid siege to Brough Castle and fierce battles were fought. An ancient ballad tells of the legendary bravery of one knight from Brough who defended the tower alone after his comrades had fallen. He was finally vanquished when the Scottish army set fire to the tower, but the incident was so dramatic that it went into the realms of storytelling and was remembered in the ballad of the Valiant Knight of Brough. This was another castle that was restored by the remarkable Lady Anne Clifford in 1650. The castle, with its tall keep, is now under the ownership of English Heritage and is well worth visiting, if only for the superb panorama of the surrounding fells to be seen from the battlements.

MARKET BROUGH is also an ancient settlement and was particularly important in the 18th and 19th centuries when it became a major coaching-town on stage-coach routes between England and Scotland. It was on the junction of several routes and boasted more than ten inns. However, the width and breadth of its High Street also indicates its importance as a market town. It was granted a charter in 1330 enabling it to hold a weekly market as well as four cattle markets and an annual fair.

One custom still celebrated in Brough is the **TWELFTH NIGHT HOLLY BURNING**, a unique festival with pagan origins. Spend some time exploring Brough; look for the beautiful 17th century carved lintel of **THE GRAPES INN** and a delightful, hidden **PACK HORSE BRIDGE** near Mill House.

To the east of Brough, STAINMORE PASS carries the A66 through a remote area of the North Pennines described by David Bellamy as 'England's last wilderness'. Here you will find the historic **PUNCH BOWL**, an 18th-century former coaching inn said to have been one of Dick Turpin's hideouts and there is reputedly a 250-yard escape tunnel connected to the basement.

Near Stainmore Summit are the foundations of **MAIDEN CASTLE**, a Roman fort built to guard the pass against marauders. A few yards over the Cumbrian border, into County Durham, is the stump of the ancient **REY CROSS** which was erected before AD946 and which, until 1092, marked the boundary between England and Scotland. It is thought to be the site of the battle at which the last Viking King of York and Northern England, Eric Bloodaxe, was killed following his expulsion from the city.

The distinctive, low hills that lie between Brough and Musgrave are drumlins - heaps of material deposited by the glaciers. In this area many drumlins are marked by broad, grassy ridges, remains of ancient lynchets or ploughing strips. There are some particularly interesting and relatively little known villages along this stretch of the Eden, such as SOULBY, which stands on the wide, grassy banks of Scandal Beck.

CROSBY GARRETT is dominated by the viaducts of the Settle - Carlisle railway. Local legend has it that the Devil, seeing all the stones lying ready to build **CROSBY GARRETT CHURCH**, carried them in his leather apron to the top of a nearby hill. He reasoned that, as people grew old, they would be unable to climb the hill and attend church and thus would come to him rather than go to Heaven.

Such tales apart, the church itself is said to be of Anglo-Saxon origin though the visible fabric is 12th century. Inside there are some superb carvings, particularly near the font. The church is also famous for its tunnel, or **HAGIOSCOPE**, cut through the wall to allow people in the north aisle to see the altar. Near the church gates is a tithe barn, built in the 18th century to store farm produce and given to the church as a religious tax.

WARCCOP, just off the A66 Brough to Appleby road, grew up as a crossing point on the Eden. It lies at the foot of one of the oldest bridges to cross the river, dating from the 16th century and red sandstone buildings surround the village green with its maypole in the centre. On the hills above the village are stones, cairns and the remains of what is claimed to be a druid's temple. The church of St Columbia is built outside the village on the site of a Roman camp. An interesting building in its own right, it is particularly famous for its rush-bearing ceremony which takes place in June each year. Close by is **DYKE NOOK FARM MUSEUM**, with a fine collection of heavy horses and farm animals.

GREAT ORMSIDE, further down the river, was once an important fort guarded by a pele tower. The ancient **CHURCH OF ST. JAMES**, which dates from the 11th century, occupies a site on a deep-sided defence mound. Relics of pre-Christian burials have been found in the mound, as well as a Viking sword (now in the Tullie Museum in Carlisle). A silver-gilt and enamel bowl from the 7th century has also been found. It is regarded as one of the most important pieces of Anglo-Saxon metalware to survive and is a particularly beautiful piece, richly decorated with vine-scrolls, birds and animals. The bowl is now on permanent display in the Yorkshire Museum in York.

A field path leads to LITTLE ORMSIDE with its large Cedar Tree said to have been brought back from Lebanon as a sapling by General Whitehead. On the voyage home he grew it in his hat and shared his daily ration of one pint of water with it.

GREAT ASBY, above Ormside, and just north of **GRANGE SCAR**, is a pretty village, set in a wooded hollow, through which **HOFF BECK** runs. Beside the stream is **ST. HELEN'S WELL**, walled on three sides and said never to run dry or freeze.

Nearby are the splendid alms-houses of St. Helen's, built between 1811 and 1820, and across the footbridge is **ASBY HALL**. The Hall once belonged to the Musgrave family of Edenhall and you can still see their crest and coat-of-arms above the door.

An added bonus for visitors is the delightful village pub, the **THREE GREYHOUNDS INN**, which dates from the early 1700s.

APPLEBY-IN-WESTMORLAND is the old county town of Westmorland, and one of the most delightful small towns in England. It was built by the Norman Ranulph de Meschines, in a defensive curve, protected on three sides by the loop of the River Eden and on the fourth by Castle Hill.

By the middle of the 12th century the church of St. Lawrence had been founded, a market established and burgage plots laid out behind the cottages which lined the main street. It continued to rise in importance, but in 1388 was almost completely destroyed by Scottish raiders, and then devastated by plague in 1598.

ST LAWRENCE CHURCH now dates mainly from the 14th century and much of it was restored by Lady Anne Clifford in the 17th century. In the Clifford Chapel are the beautiful alabaster effigy of Lady Anne's mother Margaret, Countess of Cumberland, and the monument to Lady Anne herself, with a lavish display of heraldry, one of her great loves. The organ, which was brought from Carlisle Cathedral in 1684, is the oldest working organ in Britain.

The main street, Boroughgate, with the church at the bottom end of it, has the black and white **MOOT HALL** of 1596 on an island site in the middle of the wide street.

Each year, during the first week of June, **APPLEBY HORSE FAIR** takes place with gypsies and dealers arriving in decorative motor and horse-drawn caravans. The trade, principally in horses, is a picturesque and colourful spectacle and the origins of the fair date to a charter granted in 1685 by James II.

The upper part of Boroughgate is lined with fine Georgian houses set back from the road. On the left there is an archway and porch with a hanging bell. Through the archway in the seclusion of a cobbled court-yard is St Anne's Hospital, almshouses founded by Lady Anne Clifford for elderly women.

Situated at the top of Boroughgate, 100yds from the Castle, is the **A BOARD INN**. This curiously named inn apparently derives its name from the board game of checkers. The older parts of the inn date back to the 14th & 15th century and timber beams from the original building have been used in the construction of the Lounge Bar. The walled area to the front of the inn has tables, chairs and sunshades which, along with the pretty hanging baskets and window canopies create an inviting ap-pearance. A good selection of bar meals are available at very reasonable prices including those for vegetarians and children. A bar speciality is the variety of Malt Whiskies, though we don't suggest trying them all. John and Joan have been owners here for nine years and will make you welcome.

A Board Inn, Boroughgate, Appleby in Westmorland.   Tel: 017683 51319

APPLEBY CASTLE, at the top of Boroughgate and overlooking the town, is as ancient as any in the Eden Valley but is one of the best preserved. It, too, was restored by Lady Anne, and her ghost is said to wander the castle, although many say she was too good to have a ghost and her soul must be in heaven. Beyond the Lodge Gates the massive Norman Keep dominates the castle, built between 1110 and 1120. The Great Hall is of special interest as it contains several paintings of the Clifford family, the most important of which is entitled simply, "The

Great Picture". The castle grounds are now a **RARE BREEDS SUR-VIVAL CENTRE** which shelters endangered species of domestic and wild animals and birds. The Keep and the grounds are open to the public in the summer months.

Appleby Castle and Rare Breeds Centre

THE GRAPES is a wonderful old inn situated overlooking a cricket pitch on the banks of the River Eden near the centre of Appleby-in-Westmorland. At one time this charming house belonged to the castle before it became a coaching inn. Today's landlords, Billy and Audrey Gilmour, recapture those far off days with a traditional warm welcome and plenty of good food and drink. Cosy and relaxing inside, there is a tasty menu of home-cooked pub food and an excellent range of real ales. All reasonably priced this is a popular place for a generous Sunday lunch.

The Grapes, The Sands, Appleby-in-WEstmorland Tel: 017683 51407

BONGATE, on the other side of the river, is the older part of Appleby, founded by the Vikings over a thousand years ago.

Many visitors will probably know of Appleby from its famous horse fair, but it is conveniently situated for the famous Settle to Carlisle railway which makes a visit to those towns or the popular market town of Skipton, a memorable alternative to driving.

Many areas can be easily reached from this historic market town where **THE ROYAL OAK INN** welcomes visitors from many parts of England and abroad year-round.

The Royal Oak Inn

It has been a coaching inn since the 1600's though parts of the building date back long before then. As you enter the inn, the oak panelling, old beams and open fires create an inviting atmosphere where you will find the staff most helpful and attentive. The nine bedrooms all have private bathrooms and are beautifully furnished in traditional style with all modern conveniences such as colour television, direct-dial telephone, clock radio, hairdryer and complimentary tea/coffee tray. You can choose one of the garden rooms which have French-windows to the back of the inn and there are, for a change, smaller single rooms. In the restaurant, a selection of fresh fish, local meat and vegetarian dishes are offered together with some unusual specialities. There's a choice of two dining rooms, one non-smoking, but you may be served in other rooms or bars if you prefer. Real ales are kept in top condition from a traditional cellar and a collection of fine wines and malt whiskies can be sampled. The proprietors, Colin and Hilary Cheyne will enjoy making your stay a happy and comfortable time.

The Royal Oak Inn, Bongate, Appleby-in-Westmorland, Cumbria.
Tel: 017683 51463 Fax: 017683 52300

COURTFIELD HOTEL stands in its own attractive gardens on the edge of Appleby. This former vicarage was built during the 19th century and has been owned and run by Alan and Alice Robinson for the past thirty years or so. These fine hosts offer a warm welcome to all their guests and provide excellent accommodation in eleven tastefully decorated letting rooms, some en-suite and all with colour TV and hot drinks facilities. There is a cosy and friendly guest lounge as well as a separate bar area, and in the pleasantly intimate dining room the Robinsons specialise in providing a varied menu of wholesome home-cooked food.

To accompany your meal you can choose from the extensive wine list which includes over twenty different wines.

Courtfield Hotel, Appleby-in-Westmorland Tel: 01768 351394

Just outside Appleby in Westmorland lies the fine Georgian residence that is **BONGATE HOUSE**. Standing in a large landscaped garden, this charming guest house, owned and run by Anne and Malcolm Dayson, has plenty to offer the holiday maker. The eight bedrooms, five of which have ensuite bathrooms, are all pleasantly decorated, have central heating, and other home comforts. As well as offering a bed and breakfast rate, Bongate House also offers evening meals and has a restaurant, residential licence, separate guest lounge and a residents bar. In the delightful grounds there is a putting green and a croquet lawn to enjoy and, with no irritating restrictions, guests are free to come and go as they please. A friendly establishment that will leave you relaxed and refreshed after your stay.

Bongate House, Bongate, Appleby in Westmorland Tel: 017683 51245

To the north of Appleby are the three settlements of Murton, Dufton and Knock with their distinctive conical hills close by, each named after its village and all with superb viewpoints.

DUFTON is a delightful, tiny hamlet, signposted off the main

Appleby-Penrith road. Behind the village of Dufton lies **DUFTON GILL**, a beautiful, secret, wooded valley through which runs a footpath. From Dufton there is a track carrying The Pennine Way that leads up to **HIGH CUP NICK**, a great horse-shoe precipice at the edge of the Northern Pennine escarpment formed by a glacial lake during the Ice Age.

MILBURN, in the shadow of the Great Dunn Fell, was built for defence against the Scots. All the houses of the village face inwards onto a rectangular green, presenting four solid walls to the outside world. The narrow entrances at the four corners were sealed each winter until 1826, leaving only narrow 'through-gangs', which could be easily blocked under attack.

GULLOM, near Milburn, may not be easy to find, since Gullom is not listed on many maps. Barely a hamlet, the total population of this tiny place is fourteen,

Returning towards the main A66 from Milburn you pass the pretty village of NEWBIGGIN, at the confluence of Milburn and Crowdundle Becks, and then KIRKBY THORE

TEMPLE SOWERBY, a little further along the A66 and about four miles from Penrith, is a picturesque village with red sandstone buildings around a green, it was once the home of the Order of Knights Templar who ruled the community until 1312. A walk through the delightful **OAK KOOD** takes you to **ACORN BANK**, an 18th century Manor House, now a National Trust property whose herb garden, with its magnificent display of both culinary and medicinal herbs, is open to the public.

The **TEMPLE SOWERBY COUNTRY HOUSE HOTEL**, an impressive and elegant establishment run by resident owners, Mr and Mrs Temple, is located in the pretty Cumbrian village of Temple Sowerby. An old Cumbrian farmhouse with Georgian additions it stands in two acres of well tended gardens and overlooks Cross Fell, the highest pack in the Pennines, renowned for its spectacular ridge walk. Decorated in a style that enhances its age and character, the hotel is full of lovely antique furniture, carefully chosen pictures and prints, and pretty ornaments. The downstairs drawing room is warm and inviting and the perfect place to relax, with comfortable chairs and an open log fire for those chilly Winter evenings. In Spring and Summer, guests often choose to enjoy a drink in the conservatory or on the terrace which overlooks the magnificent walled garden. There is also a popular tea rooms, open daily, where you can enjoy morning coffee, light lunches, afternoon teas and snacks. The talented chef, Andrew Walker, makes the home-made preserves, cakes and biscuits, as well as the mouth-watering five course dinner which is served each evening in the elegant and intimate dining room with its panelled walls and exposed beams. At the end of the day you can retire to one of the twelve excellently equipped bedrooms, two with four posters and all with en-suite bathroom. Four of the bedrooms are situated a few yards away from the main house in the converted Coach House, and two of these are on the ground floor and are suitable for the disabled. Whether as a stopping off point on a journey, or an escape from the stresses of everyday life, Temple Sowerby Country House Hotel is the perfect retreat.

Temple Sowerby Country House Hotel, Temple Sowerby, Near Penrith
Tel: 01768 361578

The road from Crosby Ravensworth to **ORTON** is one of the loveliest in East Cumbria, passing superb limestone scenery. The village itself stands below Orton Scar. Orton was the birthplace of George Whitehead (1636-1723) who, with George Fox, was one of the founders of the early Quaker movement. The church, in common with many in the Eden Valley, has a massive 16th century tower built for defence - a necessary precaution. On Orton Scar a beacon was lit to warn people to seek safety from the feared Scottish raiders.

If you are travelling on the B6260 Tebay to Appleby road or near junctions 38 or 39 on the M6, you can easily reach the village of Orton and find there the **NEW VILLAGE TEA ROOMS** for a light lunch or daytime snack.

New Village Tea Rooms

Take time to enjoy a stroll around this village with its space and charm which has a recorded history dating back to Edward 1. The Tea Rooms are in a large, attractive, old stone cottage built circa 1717, with a lovely little garden area where the country views and scents can be enjoyed. The inside is tastefully decorated with a nice cottage feel and one can spend time relaxing in the quiet atmosphere. You will certainly enjoy the home baking, much of which is from traditional family recipes. Start with morning coffee or tea and call back later for home made lunch or afternoon tea. These friendly Tea Rooms are open daily all year round and larger groups or parties can be catered for by arrangement. Well worth the small diversion.

The New Village Tea Rooms, Kirkland Cottage, Orton, Cumbria.
Tel: 015396 24886

SANDFORD. **THE SANDFORD ARMS** is situated just off the main A66 in the tiny hamlet of Sandford between Appleby-in-Westmoreland and Brough. Originally a collection of 18th century farm buildings, they have been expertly converted to create a beautiful residential inn with a bistro, restaurant, traditional tap room and lounge bar. A top of the range establishment with so much to offer, you can also expect a warm and friendly welcome from the owners Elizabeth and Hugh Dunwoodie. With a range of traditional ales and a fine choice of malts the bar is a delightful place to sit and relax with a drink in traditional comfort, surrounded by local stonework and a profusion of oak beams. The food at the Sandford Arms is well renowned locally and the menu offers a mouth-watering choice of classical English fayre with luscious puddings to follow. Finally, there are also five en-suite letting rooms with stunning views across the meadows or towards the nearby fells.

The Sandford Arms, Sandford, near Appleby Tel: 017683 51121

Approaching Penrith from the south, on the A6, you will pass through the village of CLIFTON.

From here it is only a few miles drive to the historic town of Penrith and on your way it is worth paying a visit to **DUNMALLOT HILL FORT** near Clifton for its beautiful views of Ullswater before making your way into the area covered by our next chapter.

CHAPTER THREE

The Lower Eden Valley

Brougham Hall

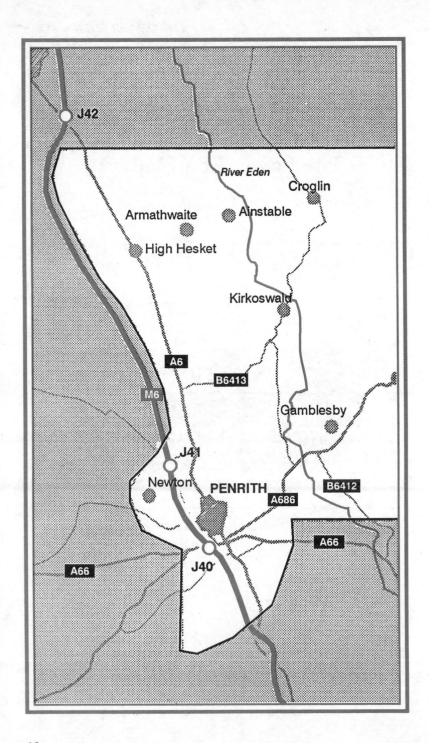

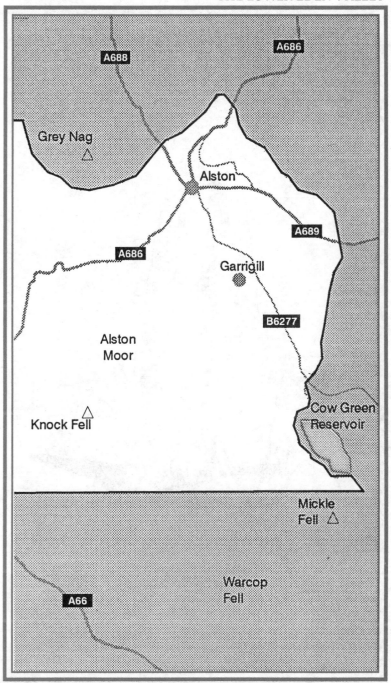

'Long Meg' Standing Stone, Little Salkeld

CHAPTER THREE

The Lower Eden Valley

PENRITH is dominated by **BEACON HILL PIKE**, which stands amidst wooded slopes high above the town. The tower was built in 1719 and marks the place where, since 1296, beacons have been lighted to warn of war and invasion. The beacon was last lit during the Napoleonic wars in 1804. It was seen by the author Sir Walter Scott who was visiting Cumberland and it prompted him to hasten home to rejoin his local volunteer regiment. It is well worth the climb from Beacon's Edge, along the footpath to the summit, to enjoy a magnificent view of the Lakeland fells.

Penrith itself is a lively market town with handsome old buildings. It is a charming mixture of narrow streets and wide-open spaces, such as **GREAT DOCKRAY** and **SANDGATE**, into which cattle were once herded during the border raids. Later they became market places and markets are still held every Tuesday and Saturday.

Penrith has a splendid Georgian church in a very attractive churchyard, surrounded by a number of interesting buildings. The oldest part of **ST ANDREW'S** dates from Norman times but the most recent part, the nave, was rebuilt between 1719 and 1772. Of particular interest is the three-sided gallery. Look out for the brass candelabra, suspended from the roof, which was a gift from the Duke of Cumberland in 1745 - a reward for the town's loyalty during the Jacobite Rising.

In the 9th and 10th centuries Penrith was the capital of Cumbria, a semi-independent state which, until AD 1070, formed part of the Kingdom of Strathclyde and Scotland. It is said that the King of Cumbria, Owen Caesarius, is buried in the churchyard amidst the group of gravestones known as **GIANT'S GRAVE**. The group consists of two ancient crosses, each 11ft high, and four 10th-century "hogback" tombstones which have arched tops and sharply sloping sides.

The ruins of **PENRITH CASTLE** bear witness to the town's important role in defending the surrounding country from marauding Scots. The castle was built around 1399, but was enlarged for the Duke of Gloucester (later Richard III) when he was Lord Warden of the Western Marches and responsible for keeping the peace along the border with Scotland. The castle has been in ruins since 1550 but remains an impressive monument.

If you are spending more than a couple of hours in Penrith, follow the **PENRITH TOWN TRAIL** which passes some of the town's historic buildings.

The first building of note on the Trail is **THE TOWN HALL**, which was the result of modernisation of two former Adam style houses, one of which was known as Wordsworth House as it was the home of the poet's cousin, Captain John Wordsworth.

Near the church is an impressive Tudor House which is now a restaurant but was, at one time, **DAME BIRKETT'S SCHOOL** attended by William Wordsworth, his sister Dorothy, and his future wife, Mary Hutchinson. The Town Trail leaflet is available at the Tourist Information Centre on Middlegate, and the trail begins from here, opposite **MUSGRAVE HALL**, which is now occupied by the British Legion but was once the home of the Musgrave family of Edenhall, and their heraldic arms are still on a lintel above the doorway.

The largest of Penrith's market spaces is known as **GREAT DOCKRAY**. On its west side is the **GLOUCESTER ARMS**, formerly Dockray Hall. It is said that the Duke of Gloucester resided here, and his coat of arms appears above the main entrance. Apparently, a secret underground passage links the Gloucester Arms with the castle.

THE COTTAGE RETREAT Tea Shop, in Burrowgate Square, lies in the heart of this old market town. The traditional cottage building, dating from the 1680s, with its low beams, has recently been restored and is a Grade II listed building. Many of the original features remain, including the old walkway at the side of the cottage building which was used by the horses for the George Hotel stable. Colin and Pamela Pollock, the owners, have, in a couple of years, created a delightful tea shop on two floors, serving traditional Cumberland dishes that, along with the cakes and pastries, are all home cooked. This certainly is a retreat from the bustle of this busy town.

The Cottage Retreat, 46 Burrowgate, Penrith Tel: 01768 863110

Situated in Angel Lane, Penrith, a busy thoroughfare full of intriguing individual shops is **THE COACH HOUSE RESTAURANT**. This olde worlde tea shop, owned and run by Valerie Woolley, compliments beautifully its surroundings. The building was originally a 19th century coaching inn and once again the weary traveller can continue his or her journey refreshed and well fed. The menu is vast with full meals and wonderful teas being a speciality and the traditional Cumberland breakfast is available all day, from 9am onwards.

Please Don't Forget...

To tell people that you read about them in

The Hidden Places

The Coach House Restaurant, Angel Lane, Penrith Tel: 01768 898032

NARROWGATE COFFEE SHOP, situated in *the narrows*, is a
hidden place well worth taking the trouble to find. Housed in a charming
refurbished building, parts of which date back to the 16th century, this
popular coffee shop offers a warm welcome and a high quality of service
and food. Of particular note is the excellent fresh ground coffee and an
incredibly wide range of fillings for its choice of delicious sandwiches
(these include hot baguettes and Italian Ciabiatta bread). This is certainly
not a 'run of the mill' coffee shop, as its popularity demonstrates.
Children are made most welcome, there are separate sections for smokers
and non-smokers, and access for wheelchair users is good. Pop in for a
visit, you will not be disappointed.

Narrowgate Coffee Shop, 13 Devonshire Street, Penrith. Tel: 01768 862599

Also in the Devonshire Arcade, in the centre of Penrith, is the newly
opened **THISTLE CRAFTS** picture gallery and gift shop. Owned and
run by Ron and Craig Garrigle this charming and interesting shop is a
super place to visit and browse around. With displays of Russian dolls,

cuckoo clocks, porcelain dolls, gifts and prints there is something for everyone. Thistle Crafts also offers a very competitive picture framing service.

Thistle Crafts, 17-19 Devonshire Arcade, Devonshire Street, Penrith
Tel: 01768 891758

Please Don't Forget...

To tell people that you read about them in

The Hidden Places

The green paintwork of **VICTORIA**, specialist clothing and gift emporium, is hard to pass without pausing a while. Situated on Castlegate, opposite Penrith Players' Theatre, the building was once a Wood's Temperance Hotel, way back in the 1890s. When Victoria Stephenson bought the shop in 1985, she found several mysterious winding staircases that led nowhere! Victoria specialises in handprinted or batik clothing usually made from natural fibres. There is a beautiful range of woodblock printed scarves in silk, cotton or chiffon. There's imaginative jewellery in silver, pewter and glass. This is sourced from diverse areas such as Western Scotland and Southern America. There's lovely spongeware from Ireland, jugs, mugs and bowls glazed in glowing colours, these depict simple tulips, roses and animals. It is a delight to use and is eagerly snapped up by its many devotees. A real treasure trove that is well worth a visit.

Victoria, 53 Castlegate, Penrith Tel: 01768 867752

Just off the centre of this market town, is Penrith's only Italian restaurant. The **DOLCE VITA RESTAURANT** is quietly situated at the rear of St. Andrew's church in Bishops Yard alongside the historic Parish Rooms. An attractive building with its light coloured exterior, the business is owned by Matteo Marras and Tosh Diliberto. The restaurant is nicely furnished and has a relaxed atmosphere. You will be given a warm greeting by Tosh who will ensure your visit is enjoyed to the full, while Matteo as Chef, cooks up some wonderful Sicilian and Sardinian specialities. You will find lots of interesting dishes on the menu all prepared to a high standard. The restaurant is open Tuesday to Saturday for lunch between 12.00 -2.00pm. and in the evening from around 5.30-10.00pm. On Sundays it is open from 6.30 to 9.30pm. and closed on Mondays. Check exact times when booking. A good choice for the good life!

Dolce Vita, Bishop's Yard, Penrith. Tel: 01768 891998

M.C.Ferguson, Ceramic Importers

M.C. FERGUSON, ceramic importers, have their shop on the main road into Penrith from the M6 motorway. Previously, the building housed 'The Gardeners', Penrith's largest grocers shop and the premises still retains the license to sell tobacco. Spanning three generations the business has undergone many changes over the years. Today, as you enter the shop, it is like entering Aladdin's cave. There are ceramic articles of every conceivable colour, style and use. Floor and wall tiles, baths, sanitary ware, fittings, garden furniture, statues, pots, fire surrounds and stoves, to mention a few. Owned and run by father and son, Mark and Adam Ferguson, this is the place to come to view the finest in European ceramics whether you are looking for something grand or more in the cottage-style.

M C Ferguson, 24-25 Brunswick Road, Penrith Tel: 01768 862951

LOWTHER SCOTT-HARDEN, based in Penrith, have an excellent and varied selection of apartments, cottages and houses available for self-catering holidays. Located throughout the Lake District and surrounding area, all the properties are fully equipped and offer a pleasant and relaxing holiday base for everyone. Much of the accommodation is set in its own grounds, with glorious views of the Lakeland scenery and several of the properties have lake access. Lowther Scott-Harden take great pride in ensuring all their customers have a wonderful time and offer a friendly and helpful service.

Lowther Scott-Harden, 4 St Andrew's Churchyard, Penrith
Tel: 01768 864541

Situated on the western bluff of the B6262, about 1 mile south of Penrith, is the magnificent **BROUGHAM HALL**. Once nicknamed 'the Windsor of the North', this is an impressive Cumbrian mansion dating back to medieval times which, in its heyday, was one of the North West's most spectacular buildings, with 39 bedrooms, a 12,000 book library, a fabulous collection of antique furniture and a Norman corridor painted with a copy of the Bayeux Tapestry.

Brougham Castle

The Hall and estate have been restored to its former glory. The restored buildings are being converted into a variety of workshops and museums, including a Children's Educational Lakeland Museum in the Tudor Hall, and in the 17th century guard house, a shop selling ceramics based on 19th century designs, and a museum commemorating the 1745 Battle of Clifton Moor, which was fought in the meadows beneath the Hall.

Brougham Hall is open all year and visitors are welcome to visit the various workshops which are already on site. These include a Smoke House, which supplies local outlets with smoked game, meat, cheeses and fish, also a hand made chocolate factory, goldsmith, jeweller, art metalworker, cabinet-maker, woodturner and stonemason. All sell their goods on site, so you can watch them at work and purchase a memento of your visit.

Brougham Hall, Brougham, Penrith 01768 68184

Nearby **BROUGHAM CASTLE**, in a most picturesque setting on the banks of the River Eamont, is where Lady Anne Clifford died in 1676. This was another of her restoration projects; in earlier times the castle had been one of the most formidable in the Eden Valley, and defended the road across the Pennines from York to Carlisle. The castle is now preserved by English Heritage, and is one of relatively few that is open all year (but not on Mondays in winter). It also houses an interesting, small exhibition of Roman tombstones from the nearby fort.

Bell Mount Farm

BELL MOUNT FARM, just two miles from the centre of Penrith, commands an wonderful position from which the surrounding countryside can be surveyed. This is a working dairy farm and from the large, square farmhouse, built in 1857, Mrs Batey offers bed and breakfast accommodation. The two guest bedrooms are large with tea and coffee making facilities, TV and radio; there is also an attractive guest sitting room. The lawned, walled garden overlooks the grazing fields and meadows of the farm. In these quiet, comfortable and friendly surroundings you will be sure to have a relaxing time. The golf driving range next door and the excellent walking country close to hand provide the opportunities to exercise off the hearty farmhouse breakfast.

Bell Mount Farm, Mill Lane, Penrith Tel: 01768 862539

EAMONT BRIDGE. THE CROWN is situated in this small village which is situated just a few minutes from Penrith. Originally a coaching inn, dating back to 1707, The Crown is close to Mayburgh Henge (a druid's stone circle), Lowther Park, Wetheriggs Pottery and Lake Ullswater. Your hosts, Wendy and Gordon, offer a warm and friendly welcome at this delightful inn.

Inside the inn, the decorations and furnishings are in keeping with the date of the building and the large open fireplace in the bar area came from Brougham Castle. With a separate restaurant, this is an ideal place to stop for a meal. The food, recently recommended in the Carlisle Good Food Guide, is just the thing after a long walk in Lakeland or as a break in a long journey on the nearby M6 motorway. For the children there is a special room and plenty of swings and slides outside in the garden.

Accommodation is available in a number of pleasant, cosy rooms with full English breakfast in the morning. Wendy and Gordon also have coarse fishing rights on the River Eden which can be used by the guests.

The Crown, Eamont Bridge, Penrith Tel: 01768 892092

NEWTON REIGNY, two miles north west of Penrith is an attractive hamlet which can be found midway between Junctions 40 and 41 to the west of the M6.

LANGWATHBY - its name meaning 'the settlement by the long ford', is situated two miles northwest of Penrith. Two prehistoric pathways cross here but the actual name of the village and of its neighbouring settlements suggest a Viking past.

Langwathby has a huge village green which still hosts *MAYPOLE DANCING* on the third Saturday in May. The green is medieval in origin and would once have been surrounded by wood and mud houses, perhaps to protect cattle but also for defence against border raids. After the Civil War and the growth in prosperity in the late 17th century, these were replaced by stone buildings. The drovers from Scotland passed through here to the market towns of England.

Once used as a grain mill and later as a drovers' inn, where, while driving their flocks from as far afield as Alston, travelling southwards towards Appleby and beyond, drovers would stop off at **BECK MILL** for a jug of warm ale and perhaps a meal around the log fire. John and Pauline MacDonald bought Beck Mill in 1990 long after the mill ceased to exist, and transformed the ruined buildings into a lively and extremely tasteful art and craft gallery known as **BECK MILL GALLERY;** it also incorporates a bespoke picture framing department and homely wholesome tea room. The gallery has a light and airy feel with a large picture window at one end. It is heated and well lit with displays of original paintings, etchings and limited edition prints with examples by many celebrated local artists. Also featured are sculptures, ceramics and individually hand crafted gifts. You will certainly enjoy a visit to this pretty gallery. From Langwathby, go under the bridge and turn right at *Kirkland* signpost, after one mile turn left at *gallery* sign.)

Beck Mill Gallery, Beck Mill, Langwathby, Penrith, Cumbria.
Tel: 01768 881371.

EDENHALL is on the opposite side of the river and is notable for its **CHURCH OF ST. CUTHBERT**. It is said that the Jarrow monks, fleeing from the Viking raids on the east coast, briefly stopped here with St Cuthbert's body before continuing their seven year wanderings. He was finally brought to rest in Durham Cathedral in AD882. Part of the church appears to be pre-Norman though most of it dates from the 12th century.

Nearby is the **PLAGUE CROSS** which stands where there was once a basin filled with vinegar. This acted as a disinfectant into which plague victims put their money to pay for food from the people of Penrith. The 16th century plague killed a quarter of the village's inhabitants.

Edenhall is particularly famous for the story of the luck of Eden

Hall, once the home of the Musgrave family, now demolished. It refers to a 13th century chalice of enamelled and gilded glass. The chalice is thought to have come from Syria and may well have been brought back by a Crusader. It was a treasured heirloom of the Musgraves for many centuries and is now in the Victoria and Albert Museum in London. According to legend, during a party the family butler went to draw water from nearby **ST CUTHBERT'S WELL** where he found a group of fairies dancing and holding court. When disturbed, they fled, leaving behind the chalice which the butler refused to return to them. As the fairies departed they cursed: *"If ever this cup shall break or fall, Farewell the luck of Eden Hall"*.

TEMPLE SOWERBY. The **KING'S ARMS HOTEL** is found conveniently situated on the main A66 road in the village of Temple Sowerby between Appleby and Penrith and on the fringe of the Lake District. A wonderful old inn of attractive red brick the King's Arms Hotel is owned and personally run by Dorothy and Malcolm Allen and offers comfortable accommodation in a choice of ten charming letting rooms, most of which have en-suite bath or shower rooms. Warm and friendly, the hotel is an ideal place to make your holiday base whilst touring this scenic area of Cumbria or fishing on the nearby River Eden.

The Kings Arms Hotel, Temple Sowerby Tel: 017683 61211

Crossing the A686 Penrith to Alston road, and following the course of the River Eden, on the north side is a pretty village called **WINSKILL**, on the road to Little Salkeld and here you cross the path of the Settle-Carlisle railway once again.

LITTLE SALKELD is a fully operational mill powered by a water-wheel. The mill specialises in producing organic, stone-ground flour which is sold locally. It is a short walk by lane from the village to **'LONG MEG AND HER DAUGHTERS'**, a most impressive pre-historic site and one of the largest neolithic stone-circles in the country.

Local legend claims that Long Meg was a witch who, with her daughters, was turned to stone for profaning the Sabbath, as they danced wildly on the moor. The circle is supposedly endowed with magic so that

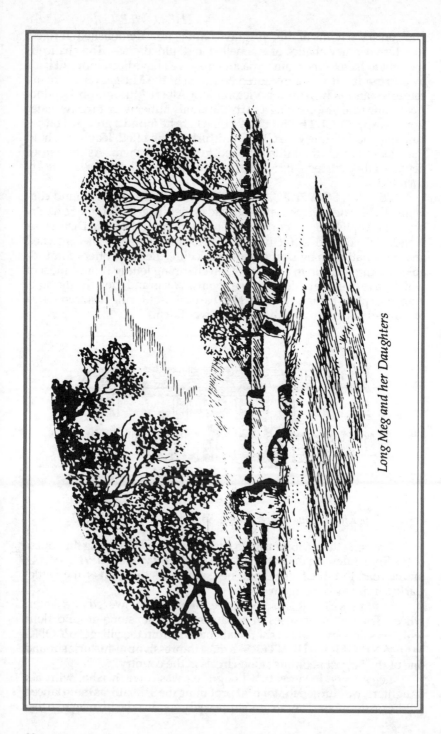

Long Meg and her Daughters

it is impossible to count the same number of stones twice. Another superstition is that Long Meg will bleed if the stone is chipped or broken. The actual name, Long Meg, has been the subject of debate. It has been suggested that 'meg' may simply be a corruption of the word 'magus', meaning a magician.

There are about sixty stones in the oval, which is approximately 300ft across. The tallest, **LONG MEG**, is a 15ft column of Penrith sandstone, the corners of which face the four points of the compass. Cup-and-ring symbols and spirals are carved on this stone which is over 3500 years old. The circle is now known to belong to the Bronze Age, but no-one is certain of its purpose. It may have been used for rituals connected with the changing seasons since the midwinter sun sets in alignment with the centre of the circle and Long Meg herself.

In 1725 an attempt was made by Colonel Lacy of Salkeld Hall to use the stones for mile-posts. However, as work began, a great storm blew up and the workmen fled in terror believing that the Druids were angry at the desecration of their temple.

BANK HOUSE FARM is situated in the quiet and peaceful village of Little Salkeld beside the River Eden. Owned by Anne and Maurice Barnes, the farmhouse, which dates back to 1700, has been tastefully renovated throughout and is full of character and charm with many of the original oak beams still exposed. The house has three bedrooms for guests all with tea and coffee making facilities one of which is suitable for disabled guests. Breakfast is served in the spacious farm kitchen which has an old oak dresser full of blue and white china and a super Aga cooker from which the fresh, home-cooked rolls come each morning.

Bank House Farm, Little Salkeld

It you prefer to cater for yourself, the Groom's Cottage has been converted to provide comfortable accommodation for up to six people. On two floors, there is a cosy lounge, fully fitted kitchen with dining area and three bedrooms. As one of the bedrooms and the bathroom are on the ground floor this is also suitable for disabled guests. If Maurice appears familiar you may remember him as the jockey who rode Rubstic to victory in the 1979 Grand National. From the farm Maurice now trains horses for National Hunt racing as well as keeping sheep, so there is plenty of farmyard activity all year round.

Bank House Farm, Little Salkeld Tel: 01768 881257

GREAT SALKELD is a picturesque collection of 18th century cottages and farmhouses built in the red sandstone that is such a characteristic of this area. Great Salkeld is said to be the birthplace of Dick Whittington. The village church is well known for its massive, battlemented pele tower built in the 14th century. The Norman doorway in the porch is less than a yard wide and its arch has three rows of deeply-cut zig-zags with five heads, one with a crown. The days of the drovers are recalled in the village by the name of its inn, **THE HIGHLAND DROVE**.

Lieutenant Colonel Samuel Lacy gave his name to the **LACY CAVES** further along the River Eden from Long Meg. It was he who had the five chambers carved out of the soft red sandstone, possibly as a copy of St. Constantine's Caves downstream at Wetheral. At that time it was fashionable to have romantic ruins and grottos on large estates and Colonel Lacy is said to have employed a man to live in his caves acting the part of a hermit. Alternatively, the caves may have been intended to provide a wine store; Colonel Lacy used to entertain his guests here and there were probably gardens around the caves. You can still see rhododendrons and laburnums which flower every Spring.

On the opposite bank of the river is **ST. MICHAEL'S WELL**, near the supposed site of a village called Addingham which was drowned when the river changed its course in the 12th century. The village church appears to have been an early Christian centre although Viking carvings were amongst some of the stones that were recovered from the river-bed during a drought in 1913. They are now on display at Glassonby. In the 'new' Addingham church the wooden pitch pipe and large stone cross, incised with lines for the ancient game of Nine Men's Morris, are of particular interest. Look out also for the village smithy under an oak tree on the village green and still in use.

MELMERBY is a lovely village situated midway between Alston and Penrith on the main A686 road.

Built around the 13 acre green, **MELMERBY HALL** was a defensive tower, added to in the 17th and 18th centuries. The church, with its tower, was a Victorian building, but the first known rector of the church was in 1332. Melmerby nestles at the foot of Hartside Pass, and the green is dissected by three becks. Even today, every householder in Melmerby has grazing rights on the green. Horses are grazed more commonly now, but in the past it would have been more usual to see flocks of geese - indeed, there was once a cottage industry here making pillows and mattresses from goose feathers.

Melmerby lies at the foot of the Pennines, and from here, the A686 climbs out of the Eden Valley to the east and the landscape changes suddenly. The road passes **FIEND'S FELL**, close to the highest point in the Pennine Chain which is the summit of Cross Fell, and as you climb, look behind you at superb views of the Eden Valley.

KIRKLAND HALL COTTAGES are situated at the foot of Cross Fell in 'England's Last Wilderness'. Owned and run by Ian and Lesley Howes, the cottages, which offer self-catering accommodation, have been granted the Country Landowners Award for the Best Conversion in the North of England. Surrounded by three acres of gardens and with panoramic views across the Eden Valley, the cottages varying in size but are all superbly decorated and furnished, featuring log fires and central heating. A comfortable and relaxing place to make your holiday base, it is essential to have a car and don't forget your walking boots! ETB 4 Keys HIGHLY COMMENDED

Kirkland Hall Cottages, Kirkland Hall, Kirkland, Penrith, Cumbria
CA10 1RN Tel: 01768 88295

At **HARTSIDE TOP**, 1904 feet above sea level midway between Melmerby and Alston, you will find spectacular views in every direction, this is a popular attraction for tourists and locals alike.

Did You Know...

There is a full

Town and Village Index

at the back of the book?

ALSTON is the highest market town in England, standing over 1000 ft above sea level. Alston is a town of great character with a wealth of interest and is a superb base from which to explore the whole of the North Pennines. There are fascinating old buildings, a cobbled main street and interesting shops. From the picturesque market cross narrow lanes radiate out and there are courtyards enclosed by old houses, many having outside staircases. When the houses were first built the living accommodation was upstairs and the animals were kept below. This part of Alston is known as **THE BUTTS**, a title acquired by the need of the townspeople to be proficient in archery during the times of the border raids.

Here you will discover a beautiful collection of art and crafts at **GOSSIPGATE GALLERY**. All the crafts and paintings have been created by artists from Northern England and parts of Scotland and as well as a permanent display, there are regular exhibitions throughout the year on different themes.

Gossipgate Gallery, The Butts, Alston 01434 381806

An unusual feature of Alston is the number of watermills in and around the town and the mill-race was once the central artery of the old town. At **HIGH MILL** visitors can see the enormous Smeaton water wheel.

The tall spire of **ST. AUGUSTINE'S CHURCH** is a local landmark, and its churchyard contains a number of interesting epitaphs, as well as affording wonderful views of the South Tyne Valley.

NENT FORCE, a waterfall, is where John Smeaton, builder of the Eddystone Lighthouse, built a five-mile underground canal tunnel - the Nent Force Level.

ALSTON MOOR was once the centre of an extremely important lead-mining region, one of the richest mining areas in Britain. Lead and silver were probably mined on the moor by the Romans, but it reached its peak in the early part of the 19th century when vast quantities of iron, silver, copper, zinc and other materials were mined by the London Lead Company, which employed thousands of workers at Nenthead. The quaker company was a pioneer of industrial welfare and built the model village of NENTHEAD to house the miners, introducing compulsory education, public baths and other benefits to its community.

Alston's Information Centre is in the waiting room of the town's station, now served by the **SOUTH TYNEDALE RAILWAY**. Visitors can take a scenic ride along the narrow-gauge steam railway hauled by little vintage engines, to Gilsland Halt on the Northumberland borders.

GARRIGILL, a remote, grey stone hamlet, lies in a deep ravine three miles from the source of the River Tyne at the foot of Cross Fell. It can be reached from the B6277 Barnard Castle road or by foot along the Pennine Way, four miles south of Alston. The church was refurbished in the 18th century but parts of it are over 700 years old. The bell is said to have been the dinner bell at Dilston Hall in Northumberland, in the days of the Jacobite Earls of Derwentwater.

GAMBLESBY, to the right of the A686 is an attractive and unspoilt fellside village dominated by a large village green which protected the cattle during the winter months. You can still see the village stocks, with iron shackles instead of traditional wooden ones.

The road continues along the valley, to LAZONBY where **BANKTOP HOUSE**, a listed building, is situated. The house was built in 1617. It is thought that this was originally the house of a Yeoman Farmer. The house retains all of its original 17th century oak features and has a Victorian extension, built to accomodate a family of over twenty!

Today Banktop House offers fine B & B accommodation and has a Tourist Board 2 Crown Commended rating. Two rooms are available, both are comfortable and well equipped and have en-suite facilities. The house has its own well tended gardens and grounds and is a good choice as a base for your stay in this fascinating area.

Banktop House, Lazonby, Penrith. Tel 01768 898268

KIRKOSWALD was once a thriving market town. Here you can still see a small cobbled market place and some very fine Georgian buildings. The village derives its name from the **CHURCH OF ST. OSWALD**. Oswald was the King of Northumbria who, according to legend, toured the pagan North with St. Aidan in the 7th century.

Kirkoswald also has a ruined 12th century **CASTLE**, formerly the home of the Featherstonehaugh family and, although not open to the public, it can be seen from the road and footpath. In 1210 a licence was received from King John to fortify the original structure and enclose the extensive park. The castle was later destroyed by Robert the Bruce in 1314 but was rebuilt and extended in the late 15th century. The whole site covered three acres with the courtyard surrounded by a massive wall and a main gate with a drawbridge over the moat. The castle's splendour is due to the efforts of Thomas, Lord Dacre but after his death in 1525 the panelling, stained glass and beamed ceilings were transferred to Naworth and the castle became a quarry. Today it is still protected by a wide moat and the great turreted tower rises above the remains of the vaulted dungeons.

One of Kirkoswald's most splendid buildings is **THE COLLEGE**, its name recalling the days when St. Oswald's was a collegiate church. The two-story house with its sloping-ended roof was originally built in 1540 as a pele tower and converted into the college for priests in the 1520's. The manor house opposite has a particularly attractive entrance front in sandstone, which was added in 1696.

Between the villages of Kirkoswald and Armathwaite are the **NUNNERY WALKS** which start at a Georgian house built in 1715, on the site of a Benedictine Nunnery founded during the reign of William Rufus. Narrow footpaths cut into sandstone cliffs along the deep gorge of **CROGLIN BECK** and pass through beautiful woodland to reveal exciting waterfalls. The walks are open to the public during the summer months.

CROGLIN, an unspoilt village nestling below the fells of North Cumbria, is famous for the legendary vampire that appeared here in 1895. The legend claimed that it only laid to rest after it had attacked a sleeping girl.

AINSTABLE, a quiet village is well worth seeking out, for here you will find **THE EDEN VALLEY WOOLLEN MILL**, where you can watch cloth being made.

ARMATHWAITE may be reached after a delightful walk from here along the eastern bank of the River Eden. A particularly fine sandstone bridge crosses the river in the village and from it there is a lovely view of **ARMATHWAITE CASTLE**.

CALTHWAITE is also well worth a visit. Renowned locally for the dairy which was a major source of employment for many years, this delightful village was the Royal Forest of Inglewood, a fact substantiated by the many local names such as High Oaks and Low Wool Oaks and Roe deer can still be seen here today. The appropriately named Thiefside, just east of Calthwaite, was the site of the gallows where poachers and sheep stealers were hanged.

CHAPTER FOUR

Carlisle to the Borders

Bewcastle

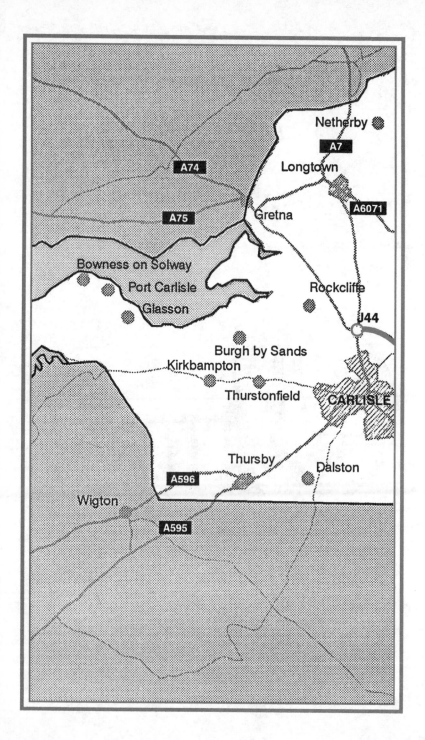

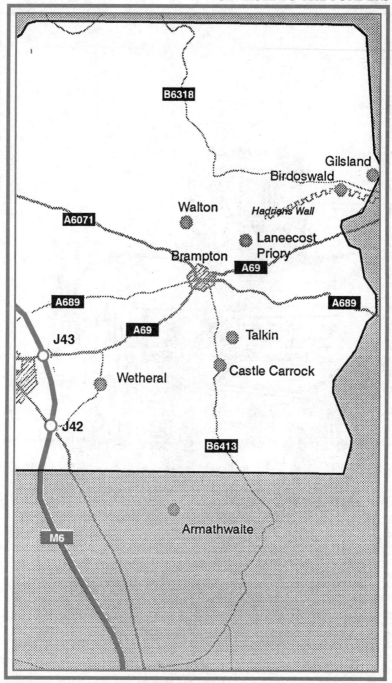

Carlisle Cathedral

CHAPTER FOUR

Carlisle to the Borders

CARLISLE and the surrounding area has changed its allegiance to Scotland and England so often in the last 800 years that many of the inhabitants could be forgiven for not knowing whether to wear the thistle or the rose. This is Border Country, a wild and lonely, evocative landscape that sets the scene for so many of Sir Walter Scott's historical novels.

But Carlisle's history is more than mere romance. This was a major strategic city on the Border, whose military past still seems to haunt it - from the Roman and Pictish battles to the skirmishes with the Scots and Jacobite rebels. There has been a castle at Carlisle at least since 1092 when William Rufus first built a palisaded fort. Almost certainly there was a fortress, probably on the present site, before Roman times, for the name 'Carlisle' comes from the Celtic 'Caer Lue', meaning 'hill fort'.

The Norman castle was originally built of wood but, during the Scottish occupation in the 12th century, King David laid out a new castle with stone taken from Hadrian's Wall. You can still see the 12th century keep enclosed by massive inner and outer walls although they have been much altered over the years.

The present **CARLISLE CASTLE** dominates the skyline of this fascinating city. Entered through a great 14th century gatehouse, complete with portcullis, and with a maze of vaulted passages, chambers, staircases, towers and dungeons, it is everything a real castle should be. Look out for the 'licking stone' and the fascinating carvings in one of the prisoners' cells showing pictures of mermaids, knights, boars and crucifixes.

Carlisle Castle was besieged for eight months during the Civil War by the Parliamentarians under General Leslie. When the Royalists finally capitulated, Leslie began repairing the castle and the walls. The Puritans were no respecters of Britain's ecclesiastical heritage; stone from six of the eight bays of the Cathedral was used for the repairs and the building of block-houses for the Puritan troops.

Partially for this reason, **CARLISLE CATHEDRAL** is now one of the smallest cathedrals in England but it has many interesting features, including an exquisite East Window, considered to be one of the finest in Europe. Below the beautifully painted wooden ceiling of the choir, with its gold star shimmering against deep blue, are the carved, canopied choir-stalls with their medieval misericords. These wonderful carved beasts and birds include two dragons joined by the ears, a fox killing a goose, pelicans feeding their young and a mermaid with a looking glass.

In the north transept is the superb 16th century Flemish 'Brougham

Triptych' which was originally in Cologne Cathedral. In the 19th century it was brought to Brougham Chapel near Penrith. The altar piece was later restored by the Victoria and Albert Museum in London and is now on permanent loan to Carlisle. It is a beautiful, intricate piece with delicately carved figures depicting scenes from the life of Christ.

It is hard to believe that this is where Edward I solemnly used bell, book and candle to excommunicate Robert the Bruce. It was here also that the church bells were rung to welcome Bonnie Prince Charlie in 1745. It is claimed that after the suppression of the Jacobite rebellion the bells were removed for their treason and only replaced in the 19th century.

Visit the **PRIOR TOWER** if you can, although an appointment is usually necessary. On the first floor of this 15th century pele tower is a wonderful forty-five panel ceiling incorporating the popinjay crest and arms of the Prior Senhouse. The 16th century Prior's gatehouse leads to a narrow lane called Paternoster which is named after the monks reciting their offices.

The award winning **TULLIE HOUSE MUSEUM,** in the centre of the city close to the cathedral, is certainly a place not to be missed; indeed, if you do nothing else in Carlisle, don't miss this place. Through skilful and interpretive techniques the fascinating, and often dark, history of the Debatable Lands, as this border region was called, is told.

Tullie House Museum and Art Gallery

The museum's centrepiece is its story of the Border Reivers who occupied the lands from the 14th to the 17th century, with a law - or rather, a lack of it - unto themselves, being neither English or Scottish, unless it suited them to pledge, unscrupulously, allegiance to one or the other. These lawless, unruly people raged inter-family warfare with each other, decimating the lives of the local people and carrying out bloodthirsty raids. Their treacherous deeds have also added such words as 'bereave' and 'blackmail' to the English language.

The horrific stories of the Reivers have been passed down through the generations in the Border Ballads, and many of the Reivers family names are still known - the museum even offers a genealogy service, so

Carlisle Cross

that you can trace your ancestry back to these people. Perhaps the definitive Reiving story has been told in 'The Steel Bonnets' by George MacDonald Fraser, author of the Flashman books.

The city of Carlisle dates back far beyond those desperate days and Tullie House also has an extensive collection of Roman remains from both the city and the Cumbrian section of Hadrian's Wall. A great Roman centre and the military base for the Petriana regiment, 'Luguvalium', as Carlisle was known in Roman times, also became a major civilian settlement with fountains, mosaics, statues and centrally-heated homes.

Tullie House Museum and Art Gallery, Castle Street, Carlisle
Tel: 01228 34781

Like many great medieval cities, Carlisle was surrounded by walls. The best view of these is in a little street called **WEST WALLS** at the bottom of **SALLY PORT STEPS**, near the **TITHE BARN**. The walls date from around the 11th century and remained virtually intact until the 19th century. When the castle was under siege, the Sally Port allowed an individual to 'sally forth'. It was later used for access to the Tithe Barn to avoid paying city tolls. It is unusual to find a tithe barn within a city wall but this exception was probably made because of the Border raids. The barn dates from the 15th century and was used to collect and store taxes, or tithes, destined for the priory.

Close by is **ST CUTHBERT'S CHURCH**, the official city church of Carlisle, housing the Lord Mayor's pew. Although the present building dates from 1778, there has been a church of St Cuthbert on this site since the 7th century. St Cuthbert was Bishop of Carlisle in AD680. It is a charming Georgian building with several interesting features including a moveable pulpit on rails.

THE OLD TOWN HALL, now an excellent Tourist Information Centre, dates from the 17th century and once housed the 'MUCKLE BELL', an alarm bell which, it was claimed, could be heard eleven miles away. The bell is now housed in the Tullie House Museum.

The **GUILDHALL MUSEUM** is housed in an unspoiled medieval building constructed by Richard of Redeness in 1407. Originally a town house it provides an ideal setting for illustrating the history of both the Guilds and the City. Several rooms are devoted to creating the atmosphere of trade Guilds such as the shoe-maker, the butcher and the glover. There is a splendid early 19th century banner of the weavers Guild and an impressive collection of 17th/18th century Guild silver. Displays also feature other items relating to the history of Carlisle and include a magnificent iron-bound Muniment Chest dating from the 14th century. Conducted tours of this remarkable Guildhall are available using a 'Time Machine' audio guide.

Guildhall Museum, Castle Street, Carlisle Tel: 01228 34781

Not far from the museum is the **CITADEL RAILWAY STATION**.

Carlisle Castle

Carlisle Guildhall Museum

The first railway to Carlisle opened in July 1836 and Citadel Station, which opened in 1850, was to house seven different railway companies whose coats of arms are still displayed on the facade. So elegant was its interior - and much of it remains - that Carlisle was known as the 'top hat' station. Today it is still an important station; Intercity trains from Glasgow and London now link with lines to Dumfries, Tyneside, West Cumbria and Yorkshire, and it is, of course, the northern end of the famous Settle-Carlisle Railway line.

The line of **HADRIAN'S WALL** runs through Carlisle following the northern rim of the River Eden. The Wall was built as a great military barrier across the narrowest part of Britain, from the mouth of the Tyne in the east to Bowness-on-Solway in the west. Guarded by forts at regular intervals, it was built between AD122-128 following a visit by the Emperor Hadrian who saw the military infra-structure as insufficient to withstand the combined attacks of northern barbarians. Originally much of the western side was built from turf, but by AD163 this had been replaced by stone. The wall was finally abandoned in the late 4th century.

Carlisle has many good restaurants and wine bars. One of the very best is hidden away, but it is well worth seeking out. **ZAPOTEC**, a Mexican and Spanish restaurant, is situated in one of the oldest parts of Carlisle in the cellar of a Georgian building. This well renowned restaurant, owned and personally run by Jan Huddart and David Taylor, is characterful and atmospheric. The menu features many excellent and interesting dishes from the two countries including a delicious array of tasty Tapas that can be eaten at any time. Authentic Mexican food, rather than Tex Mex hybrids, the menu is a wonderful mix of flavours, not all hot, that has something for everyone. Naturally, cocktails and sherry feature on the list of aperitifs but Zapotec's also has an excellent range of bottled beers and wines. A very popular restaurant, it is best to book at busy times.

Zapotec, 18 Fisher Street, off Long Lane, Carlisle
Tel: 01228 512209 Fax: 01228 539100

Around Carlisle

Some of the best remains are to be seen at BIRDOSWALD, a Roman fort that guarded the bridge carrying the Wall over the River Irthing at Willowford. Birdoswald is set high on a plateau with magnificent views over the surrounding landscape. The fort has a particularly well preserved eastern gate. It would originally have covered five acres and may have been the base for 500 cavalry or 1000 foot soldiers. The site at Birdoswald is now open to the public. It belongs to English Heritage, who have carried out much excavation work and opened a Visitor Centre which brings the history of this site to life, from the early Roman days, through the middle ages and the border raids, to the romanticism of the Victorians. In 1850 Henry Norman, an enthusiastic archaeologist, extended the farmhouse, built the tower and began the excavation works to the fort walls and gates. Recent excavations have uncovered the fort's granaries and west gate with evidence of early post Roman occupation. Birdoswald is unique; at no other point along Hadrian's Wall can all the components of the Roman Frontier system be seen in such a small area. A fine stretch of the Wall runs from Birdoswald to **HARROW'S SCAR MILECASTLE** which stands at the top of a steeply-wooded slope overlooking the river.

GILSLAND, East of Birdoswald is where one of the best preserved milecastles on the Wall may be found. Standing on a grassy slope above **POLTROSS BURN**, it is 10ft high in places. Gilsland is also known for its sulphur spring and there was once a convalescent home for miners and shipyard workers here. It is now owned by the Co-operative Society and people still drink the waters as a cure for arthritis and rheumatism. Near the spring is **THE POPPING STONE**, traditionally where a man popped the question to his lover. It was here that Sir Walter Scott successfully proposed to Charlotte Carpenter.

HIGH CROSBY. **CROSBY LODGE** has the appearance of one of those lovely country house estates seen in classical television drama productions, its great charm and character would certainly fit well with the romantic image portrayed in such presentations.

Crosby Lodge

Twenty five years ago, the resident owners Michael and Patricia Sedgwick had the unenviable task of converting this mansion from a dilapidated and seriously neglected building to the present romantically beautiful **COUNTRY HOUSE HOTEL AND RESTAURANT** with large spacious rooms, elegantly furnished and appointed to provide the maximum of comfort. Crosby Lodge is perfect for a quiet, relaxed vacation where the family maintain a very high standard of personal attention and service. All the bedrooms have private bathrooms and are luxuriously appointed. The Restaurant menus offers exceptional variety and a wide choice of traditional British fare and authentic Continental cuisine. A lighter selection of lunchtime snacks is also available in the Restaurant and in the Cocktail Bar. With its spacious grounds and walled garden, Crosby Lodge has the perfect setting for parties, anniversaries weddings and social events. Carlisle and the M6 motorway are only few miles away. ETB - 4 Crowns Highly Commended.

Crosby Lodge, High Crosby, Crosby-on-Eden, Carlisle, Cumbria.
Tel: 01228 573618 Fax: 01228 573428

BRAMPTON. Following the course of the River Irthing back towards Carlisle, two miles north east of Brampton is **LANERCOST PRIORY**, an impressive red sandstone ruin set in secluded woodland. The Priory was founded in 1166 by Robert de Vaux and built largely of stone from the Roman Wall. During 1306, Edward I spent six months at the Priory recuperating after his skirmishes with the Scots. Lanercost is well preserved and its scale is a reminder that it was a grand complex in its heyday. However, the Priory suffered greatly in the Border raids of the 13th and 14th centuries. It was finally disbanded at the Dissolution of the Monasteries but in 1740 the ruined nave was restored to form what is now one of the most splendid parish churches in the country. It is worth going inside to admire the William Morris glass.

The Abbey Bridge Inn

The **ABBEY BRIDGE INN** occupies a quiet, peaceful riverside setting near Lanercost Priory, just two miles from the pleasant market town of Brampton. Dating back to the 1850s, the hotel, which is owned and personally run by the Sayers family, has an interesting history. Originally a farmhouse, it later became an ale house and, under the influence of the Countess of Carlisle, a Temperance Inn in 1900. The Abbey Bridge Inn incorporates the old Blacksmiths Forge (c.1640) which has been refurbished and is now an attractive bar and galleried restaurant. Voted *the Best Real Ale Pub in Cumbria* in 1992 by CAMRA, and the winner of many subsequent awards, you can be sure of an excellent choice of real ales. The restaurant is a superb setting for a quiet intimate meal. All the food is prepared from fresh market produce with vegetarians give special consideration. Finally the inn also has seven charming and delightful letting rooms that make this a wonderful place to stay with a real family feel.

The Abbey Bridge Inn, Lanercost, Brampton CA8 2HG Tel: 016977 2224

Brampton actually dates back as far as the 7th century, and was originally sited a mile north west of its present position. On the departure of the Romans from the area, the settlement grew. The present town was created by Thomas de Multon, Lord of Gilsland, in the early 13th century. The octagonal **MOOT HALL** in the market place, with its handsome clock tower, is Brampton's most striking building. It is also where you will find the Tourist Information Centre, on the upper floor. The present hall was built in 1817 by Lord Carlisle but there has been a Moot Hall here since 1648. The iron stocks at the foot of a double flight of external stairs were last used in 1836.

The Nag's Head Inn

THE NAGS HEAD INN stands across from the market place in this historic town. The late 17th century building was originally much smaller and was known as the Horse Head Inn. It was changed to the Nags Head in the late 18th century but history does not give a reason why. Present-day hosts are Tony and Pam Hawkins who took over the inn twelve months ago after a move from the West Midlands. The inn caters during normal opening hours at lunchtime and in the evening where anything from freshly cut sandwiches to a 12oz T-Bone steak may be enjoyed. As you would expect, there is plenty of character in this building and being situated in a market town, there is always some good conversation to be had with the local residents and business people. Two bedrooms are available for guests which makes for a friendly and enjoyable stopover whilst touring the area.

The Nags Head Inn, Market Place, Brampton, Cumbria.   Tel: 016977 2284

Just off the market square is **ST MARTIN'S CHURCH** which was rebuilt in 1878. It was designed by Philip Webb, a member of the pre-Raphaelite brotherhood, who requested that stained glass should be installed. Climb up to the wooded mound for a magnificent view of the Solway Plain and the distinctive Scottish mountains on the Galloway coast.

OAKWOOD PARK HOTEL, on Longtown Road, just outside Brampton, makes an excellent base for touring the Borders, and the Lake District and is situated within a mile of Hadrian's Wall. Standing in secluded grounds. This impressive Victorian residence provides comfortable accommodation in five en-suite guest rooms all with TV and hot drinks facilities. The ambience is warm and welcoming with open log fires in the dining room and drawing room. There is a cosy lounge bar where guests can relax with a drink in an un-hurried atmosphere before sampling the excellent traditional cuisine.   A convenient centre for visiting the beautiful English Lakes and the peaceful hills of the Borders and Southern Scotland. ETB- 2 Crowns. AA - QQQQ

Oakwood Park Hotel, Longtown Road, Brampton, Cumbria.
Tel: 016977 2436

SANDS HOUSE HOTEL, standing on the edge of the historic and picturesque market town of Brampton, is owned and personally run by Pauline and Geoff Cashmore. A 17th century former coaching inn, this old building has lost none of its character and charm even though it has been completely modernised over the years and many of the originally features have been retained.

Sands House Hotel has 12 superior en-suite guest bedrooms that are all tastefully decorated and furnished and one has been specifically equipped with the disabled guest in mind. Open all day, everyday, delicious, home-cooked meals are available at lunchtime and in the evening and the bar is stocked with a range of excellent well kept real ales such as Boddingtons, Theakstons and Old Speckled Hen.

Sands House Hotel, The Sands, Brampton Tel: 01697 73085

KIRKLINTON. **CLIFTHOUSE FARM** lies at Kirklinton, just off the main A6071 Longtown to Brampton road. Built in 1909, the farmhouse is part of a working 136 acre sheep and cow farm owned and run by Margaret and Bill Harrison. Bill has lived and worked the farm for over 50 years and for the past 16 years the couple have been offering first class bed and breakfast accommodation from their spacious house. There are five comfortable, well decorated and furnished letting rooms and you can expect a hearty farmhouse breakfast each morning. Evening meals can be provided by prior arrangement. This is a delightful spot on the banks of the River Lyne and coarse fishing is available close by.

Clifthouse Farm, Kirklinton, Carlisle Tel: 01228 75237

HETHERSGILL. Thought to be nearly 400 years old, the **POINTER DOG INN** at Hethersgill is a meeting-point for the local farming community as well as being the starting place for the district fox-hunt.

Debra, along with help from parents Glenda and Malcolm, are hosts at the inn which has a good mix of locals and visitors. This is a good old-fashioned English pub situated about a mile from the centre of the village with panoramic views in every direction. The 'Pointer' offers a good range of ales including Yougers Scotch, Tetleys and Boddingtons, together with a great bar snack menu. In winter the inn is closed at lunchtime Monday to Friday but is open all day Saturday and Sunday.

The Pointer Dog Inn, Bolton Fell, Hethersgill, Carlisle, Cumbria.
Tel: 01228 75406

South of Brampton are **GELT WOODS**, lying in a deep, sandstone ravine carved by the fast-flowing River Gelt. By the river is an inscribed rock called **WRITTEN ROCK** which is thought to have been carved by a Roman Standard Bearer in AD207.

From Gelt Wood it is a delightful walk to **TALKIN TARN**, where the lake in the Country Park has been popular for water-sports for over 100 years. Legend has it that beneath the surface of the lake there is a submerged village destroyed by a wrathful god and that in certain light you can still see the ruins below.

The Hare and Hounds Inn, Talkin

TALKIN. Enjoying a charming location in the lovely Cumbrian village of Talkin, you will find the **HARE AND HOUNDS INN.** This historic 18th century coaching house was once used as a stop-over by

Talkin Tarn Country Park

monks on their way from Armathwaite to Lanercost Priory. This is a welcoming establishment where you can sample fine cask-conditioned ales and tasty home-cooked meals; the menu offers a very good selection including vegetarian and children's dishes plus blackboard specials. The Tarn Lounge provides a cosy relaxing atmosphere with exposed beams, open fires and soft lighting. The Coats of Arms Bar is a special feature with stained glass windows around the bar. At the end of the day, you can retire to one of the comfortable guest rooms, one of which has a four-poster bed. Open throughout the week in the evenings (daytime during school holidays), and all day Saturday and Sunday.

The Hare & Hounds Inn, Talkin Village, Nr. Carlisle, Cumbria.
Tel: 016977 3456

CASTLE CARROCK, a little further south lies among beech trees below the fells with an old pub and stone cottages. An ancient settlement, archaeologists have found several pit-dwellings in the hills above the village and a skeleton of a man with a drinking cup in a cairn at Greenwell.

The Duke Of Cumberland Inn

'*A hidden gem*' truly describes **THE DUKE OF CUMBERLAND INN** which is situated in the scenic village of Castle Carrock, near Brampton, and overlooked by the Fells. At first glance the inn looks more like a private house and indeed has, in its varied 120 year history, reverted to and from private dwelling. It faces out over a small village green with the church beyond. Owned and personally run by Nora Little for the past few years, the inn oozes character and charm. It is tastefully decorated and furnished and Nora will always give you a warm and friendly welcome. An ideal place to aim for to have a tasty home cooked meal in the newly restyled dining area or enjoy a delicious bar meal and one of four excellent real ales, by a roaring log fire. There is a very good menu selection and 'specials' listed on the blackboard.

Food served daily except Mondays. Families are welcome.

The Duke of Cumberland Inn, Castle Carrock, Carlisle, Cumbria.
Tel: 01228 70341

WETHERAL lies between Castle Carrock and Carlisle, above the River Eden, over which runs an impressive railway viaduct carrying the Tyne Valley Line.

WETHERAL PARISH CHURCH lies below the village beside the river and contains a sculpture by Joseph Nollekens, of the dying Lady Mary Howard clasping her dead baby. St Constantine was the local patron and the church is dedicated to the Holy Trinity, St Constantine and St Mary. Constantine died as a martyr in AD657 and a life-sized statue of him can be seen in the grounds of CORBY CASTLE.

During the reign of William Rufus one of his barons, Ranulph Meschin, founded a priory for Benedictine monks at Wetheral above the red-rock gorge of the River Eden. It was a dependency of the Abbey of St Mary at York and the Prior and the monastery served the church and domestic chapel of Corby Castle. All that remains now is the gatehouse, but the grounds of Corby Castle are open to the public and provide some very pleasant woodland walks.

SCOTBY. THE ROYAL OAK is a lovely country pub situated in the old Quaker village of Scotby, just a couple of miles from Carlisle City centre. Dating back to the early 19th century, this old building has plenty of character and charm. A cosy pub, popular with locals and visitors, much of its warm and friendly atmosphere is generated by the hosts Angela and Anthony Naisbitt. As well as serving an excellent pint of real ale, the Royal Oak is also popular for its wonderful, home-cooked food which is available at both lunchtimes and evenings. There is always something going on here and it is a super place to drop into at any time.

The Royal Oak, Scotby, Carlisle Tel: 01228 513463

ROCKLIFFE. THE CROWN AND THISTLE is a real gem of a public house and restaurant, situated in a secluded spot in the pictur-esque village of Rockliffe; here you can feel miles away from the hustle and bustle of daily life yet the centre of Carlisle is only ten minutes drive. Hosts Tony and Pam are local people and have plenty of experience in the trade. The Crown and Thistle was originally three cottages dating from around the early 18th century and it is believed that the conversion to an Inn occurred about 100 years ago. The interior is very nicely decorated in keeping with the style and period. The delicious food in prepared and cooked by Pam and the daily menus are written up on a large blackboard. A good choice of well kept ales include Scotch, 70 Bitter, Theakstons, plus a guest beer and non- alcoholic on draught. Well worth a visit.

The Crown & Thistle, Rockliffe, Carlisle, Cumbria.   Tel: 01228 74044

BRISCO. CROSSROADS HOUSE is set in open countryside near the village of Brisco, just three miles south of Carlisle and near its racecourse.

Crossroads House

Formerly two cottages dating back to the early 19th century and once part of the historic Woodside estate, this charming country guest house, owned and personally run by Anne and Neville Jennings, offers warm and friendly hospitality to all visitors. There are five comfortable bedrooms which vary in size from single rooms to large family rooms. Crossroads believes that everyone should start the day with a hearty breakfast and this is indeed what is served to all in the guests dining room, adjacent to the lovely conservatory, with its panoramic views of the Pennines and the Northern Lakeland fells. The delicious meal is the perfect way to start the day, particularly if you are going to spend it out exploring the wonderful countryside.

Crossroads House, Brisco, Carlisle Tel: 01228 28994

DURDAR. The impressive **BLACK LION INN** holds a prominent position in the tiny hamlet of Durdar, near Carlisle. Dating back to the 1930s, this interesting and unusual building was formerly part of the Carlisle estate but it became freehouse some years ago.

For the passed eighteen months, the Black Lion Inn has been run by Anita and David Wren. Well known locally, this is a popular place where you can be sure to find excellent food and drink as well as a warm and friendly welcome. The ale is kept in tip top condition and the pub features Theakston's and Younger's Scotch along with occasional specials. Whether you choose your meal from the listed menu or from the daily specials board you can be sure of a delicious and tasty, home-cooked meal. This is a lovely, relaxed and friendly inn that is a great credit to your hosts, Anita and David.

Black Lion Inn, Durdar, Carlisle Tel: 01228 20931

KIRKBY MOOR COUNTRY HOUSE HOTEL AND RESTAURANT is set in two and a half acres of magnificent private grounds just outside the village of Brampton. A grand and charming Victorian country house, with plenty of character, the hotel is owned and personally run by Judy and David Green.

With an interesting history of its own, Kirby Moor is probably more famous for the crash of a Lancaster bomber here in 1943. Returning from a mission over Germany in January 1943, the bomber overshot the airfield near Carlisle and crash landed in a field half a mile from the hotel. Showering wreckage over a wide area, many outbuildings were set on fire and only two of the aircraft's crew of seven survived the holocaust. Today, the hotel offers peace and tranquillity surrounded by splendid scenery. There are six comfortable and beautifully furnished bedrooms all with either en-suite or private bathrooms. The restaurant, a recent addition, lies adjacent to the main hotel building and is a wonderful place for a superb, well-prepared meal and the excellent list of fine wines goes to make your meal a really special occasion.

Kirby Moor Country House Hotel and Restaurant, Longtown Road, Brampton Tel: 016977 3893 Fax: 016977 41847

WARWICK is well worth visiting for here you will find the remarkable Norman **CHURCH OF ST LEONARD**, which consists of a restored nave and chancel with a curiously buttressed apse and a splendid arch leading into a modern vestibule.

Warwick's other church, **ST PAUL'S**, is reputed to have been commissioned by a wealthy Carlisle man who took umbrage at a sermon preached at St Leonard's.

LONGTOWN, on the north side of Hadrian's Wall, towards the Scottish border, is the last town in England. Its position, on the River Esk and so close to the border, has influenced its history from earliest times. The Romans occupied this land, and they were followed by other conquerors. The legendary King Arthur attempted to organise the Northern Britons against the pagan hordes who tried to settle and control this territory. In the 6th century the mighty battle of Ardderyd was fought here, and according to legend, 80,000 men were slain.

Until 1750 Longtown was a small hamlet of mud-dwellings. Dr. Robert Graham, an 18th century clergyman, proposed the building of the **ESK BRIDGE**, which was completed in 1756 and it was this venture that led to Longtown's establishment as a bustling border town. These days it has some fine individual buildings and broad, tree-lined terraces of colour-washed houses.

On the outskirts of Longtown, just off the A6071, is **ARTHURET CHURCH**. The earliest records of the church date from 1150 and it was originally served by the monks of Jedburgh.

The present church, dedicated to St Michael and All Angels, was built in 1609, financed by a general collection throughout the realm, which James I ordered after a report that the people of Arthuret Church were without faith or religion. The people that he referred to, of course, were the infamous Reivers, ungoverned by either English or Scottish laws In 1745 another army marched through Longtown; this time it was Bonnie Prince Charlie and his men, making a bid for the English crown. They crossed the River Esk at RIDDINGS and stayed at **RIDDINGS HALL**.

KIRKANDREWS, to the north of Longtown is the parish long associated with the Grahams of **NETHERBY HALL**, where Sir Walter Scott wrote 'Young Lochinvar'. The grounds of the hall are sometimes opened to the public in Spring, when the daffodils are in bloom.

The beautiful church at Kirkandrews was connected to Netherby Hall by a suspension bridge, which is now privately owned. Built in 1637, it contrasts strongly with the 15th century pele tower nearby, the tower having been built for safety during the attack, whereas the church was built after peace came to the area.

PORT CARLISLE. At one time sailing boats made their way by a canal from Port Carlisle to the heart of the city of Carlisle. Boats were towed to the city (taking 1 hour 40 minutes), enabling Carlisle to be reached within a day by sea from Liverpool. The canal was later replaced by a railway which brought many Scandinavian emigrants through Carlisle on their way to the USA. The building of the Bowness railway viaduct altered the deepwater channels, causing Port Carlisle to silt up, the railway was eventually abandoned but its old course can still be traced.

The Solway Firth coast is an area of tiny villages with fortified towers standing as mute evidence to the Border struggles of long ago. These villages were the haunts of smugglers, wildfowlers and half-net fishermen. What is particularly special about this coastline is its rich birdlife.

BURGH-BY-SANDS. On 7th July 1307, the body of King Edward I was laid out in the church at Burgh-by-Sands. He was already a dying man when he left Carlisle to march against his old enemy, Robert the Bruce. A monument to Edward was erected on the marshes and a later monument still marks the spot. **THE CHURCH OF ST MICHAEL** dates from 1181 and was constructed entirely of stones from a fort on the Roman wall. Of particular interest is the fortified tower built for defence against the Border raids, which has 7ft thick walls. The tower can only be entered through a strong iron grill; this is possibly the earliest surviving example of a fortified church.

KIRKBAMPTON. The church in this lovely village, though restored in 1882, was originally Norman and let into the chancel-wall are even older stones taken from the Roman wall.

This coastline is the setting for Walter Scott's novel, 'Red Gauntlet', and the fortified farmhouse by the roadside at Drumburgh is said to be the 'White Ladies' of the novel. Further along the coast is GLASSON, an important Nature Reserve and the centre of the half-net fishing industry.

THURSTONFIELD lies five miles west of Carlisle and between 1870 and 1930 was a thriving farming and business community. Almost completely self-sufficient, the villagers grew their own fruit and vegetables and used their own wells for water. At that time, although illegal, cockfights took place in a pit alongside the Methodist chapel, originally built in 1861, which still serves a congregation today.

THURSBY, South of Thurstonfield at the junction of the A595/596, takes its name from Thor, the Saxon god of Thunder whose temple was said to have been nearby at Kirksteads.

A focal point of the village is **ST ANDREW'S CHURCH** which dominates the skyline and it is here in the graveyard that the body of Rev. Mason lies, a former curate of Thursby whose granddaughter was the famous Mrs. Beeton, writer of the classic book on *'Household Management'*.

DALSTON, lies just east of Thursby and is a delightful and unspoilt country village close to Carlisle.

Lying on the banks of the river Caldew, Dalston became a thriving cotton industry in the late 18th century, thanks to George Hodgson of Manchester, who used the river as the source of power for the flax mill and four cotton mills that were established here. The local economy was sustained still further by the emergence of a forge and two corn mills.

Also in the main square you will find **COUNTRY KITCHEN**, a traditional tea shop run by Julie Smaile where you can enjoy home cooking at its best. Country Kitchen is a cosy, friendly establishment tempting locals and tourists alike to pop in and sample the freshly baked gingerbread or Cumberland currant cake with a warming drink. There is always a soup of the day, a roast of the day, a vegetarian dish and a meat dish, all made using local produce. You can even take away with you some homemade bread, homemade cakes, biscuits, sponges etc. as a tasty memento. Open Tuesday - Saturday 10.00am - 4.30 pm. Lots of parking area in the village square.

The Country Kitchen, 5 The Square, Dalston, Carlisle, Cumbria.
Tel: 01228 711431 or 01697 478621

At the eastern end of the village square, stands **ST MICHAEL'S CHURCH**, believed to date back to Norman times, which can be approached via a memorial lychgate. One of the few red brick buildings to be found in the village is the Victorian chapel which stands somewhat hidden between several Georgian houses along the village green.

GREAT ORTON is a small town well worth taking the trouble to visit. Situated to the North of Thursby, this lovely village has a typical old English inn, **THE WELLINGTON,** which is worth seeking out . It has been a pub for about 100 years since its conversion from four cottages. By way of association, the pub sign shows a picture of the Duke of Wellington, though this is not considered to be the real connection since its name is thought to be derived from another interesting source. Under the present car park is a natural well from which, many years ago, the children from the adjacent school would draw water for the day, hence -'*The Well In Town*'. Enter The Wellington on a cold day and a roaring fire greets you along with a great welcome from Glenn and Liz the Tenants. As is customary in many inns these days, food is served lunchtimes and evenings with lots of daily specials available. And, as is also the custom, a good selection of real ales are on offer; Hartleys XB, Fell Runner, Robinsons Best and Three Shires, are regularly available here. A neat private beer garden is at the rear of the pub and proves very popular in the warmer weather. Just five miles from Carlisle city centre.

The Wellington Inn, Great Orton, Carlisle, Cumbria.   Tel: 01228 710775

CHAPTER FIVE

North Lakeland

Stonethwaite in Borrowdale

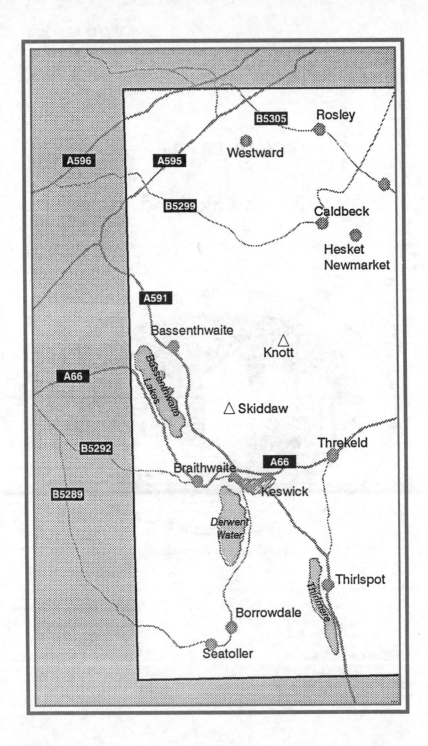

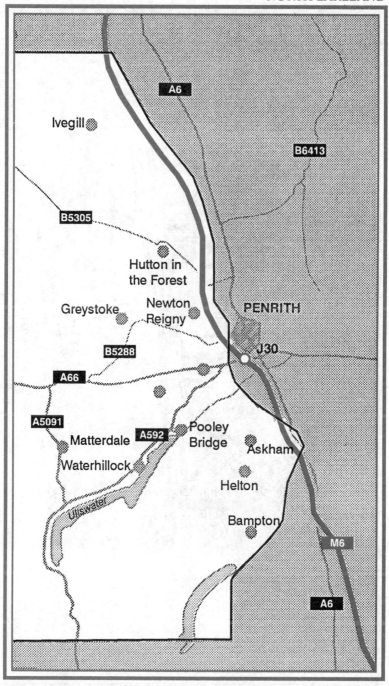

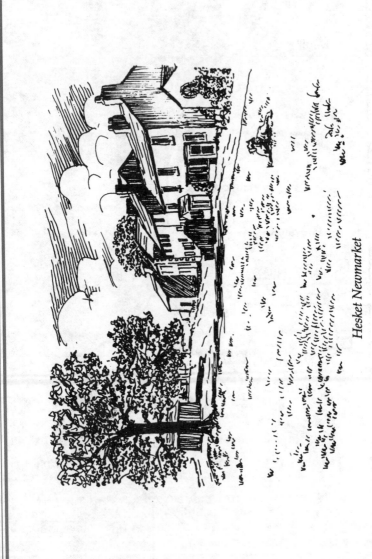

Hesket Newmarket

CHAPTER FIVE

North Lakeland

The northern Lake District, to the north, east and west of Keswick, is for many enthusiasts, classic Lakeland, the scenery dominated by the rounded, heather-clad slopes of the Skiddaw range to the north of Keswick, and the wild, craggy mountains of Borrowdale and the Central Fells to the south. But despite this area's popularity, there are many hidden places to discover which are off the beaten track.

North of Skiddaw, towards Carlisle, lies an area of countryside formerly covered by the ancient Forest of Inglewood. Now it is farmland with isolated hamlets across which a dense network of quiet lanes and trackways are spread, dotted with attractive villages such as Westward, Rosley and Ivegill.

SEDBERGHAM is the largest village, a scattered settlement containing several 18th century farmhouses. Legend says that it was founded in medieval times by a hermit - one William Wastell - who made a clearing in the forest with his four supporters and established the village.

CALDBECK is the most famous village in this area because of its associations with John Peel, the famous huntsman who lies buried in the churchyard. Peel was Master of Hounds for over fifty years and was immortalised by his friend John Graves, who worked in a local mill making the grey woollen cloth mentioned in the song, *"D'ye ken John Peel with his coat so grey?"*

With its picturesque church, village green, cricket field, pond and blacksmith's forge, Caldbeck has all the ingredients of a picture postcard village. There has been a church here since the twelfth century, one of only eight in England to be dedicated to St. Kentigern. The other seven are also to be found in the north of Cumbria, where Kentigern, a bishop in the Strathclyde area of Scotland, spent his time in exile.

Until two hundred years ago Caldbeck was an industrial village, with corn mills, woollen mills and a paper mill all powered by the river. PRIEST'S MILL, built in 1702 by the Rector of Caldbeck, next to the church, was a stone grinding corn mill, powered by a waterwheel which has now been restored to working order. It is open to the public, and has an accompanying mining museum and a collection of old rural implements. The mill buildings are home to a gift shop, craft workshops, and a tea-room - one of Cumbria's best - on the top floor.

HESKET NEWMARKET, just one mile from Caldbeck, is a peaceful and attractive village. The village is surrounded by beautiful countryside and is within easy reach of the Caldbeck Fells, Carrock Fell and The Swineside Valley.

NEWLANDS. THE SWINSIDE INN, set in the middle of the Newlands Valley is a 'hidden place' well worth finding. Here, surrounded by unrivalled countryside and some of the best walks in the Lake District you can enjoy fine ales and delicious and reasonably priced bar meals in a friendly and warm atmosphere. The ambience is complemented by the 'olde worlde' character of the interior of the inn, provided by its oak beams, stone floors and open log fires. In good weather you can take advantage of the lovely beer garden, which has over thirty tables. The owners of the inn, Alfred and Jean Fletcher and their family are justly proud of the enviable reputation that they have worked hard to build up for the inn, and visitors can be assured of receiving a warm welcome.

Swinside Inn, Newlands, Nr Keswick, Cumbria. Tel: 017687 78253

SWINSIDE LODGE HOTEL is a Victorian Lakeland house, beautifully situated in its own grounds at the foot of Catbells, a mere five minutes stroll from the shores of Derwentwater. The house has nine attractive and thoughtfully decorated bedrooms each offering a high degree of comfort and relaxation.

The Swinside Lodge Hotel

Every room has a private bathroom or shower and is equipped with central heating, colour television, radio, hairdryer, tea-making facilities and several other extras to help make your stay more enjoyable. You will be impressed with the food, a hearty Cumbrian breakfast sets you up for the day, in the evening return to a delicious, candle-lit meal. The five course set menu is changed daily and is prepared by Cordon Bleu chefs using the best local ingredients available to provide a varied and balanced menu. Dinner may include a delicious home-made soup followed by a roast with a selection of fresh vegetables. A choice of puddings and an interesting variety of British farmhouse cheeses to round off your meal before taking coffee in the sitting rooms. The Swinside Lodge Hotel is situated midway on the Portinscale to Grange road and is located by leaving the A66 Keswick to Cockermouth road at the signpost for Newlands Valley, Portinscale, Grange.

Swinside Lodge Hotel, Newlands, Keswick, Cumbria.
Tel & fax: 017687 72948

Set in beautiful countryside just 2 miles from Dewentwater and 5 miles from Keswick, **LITTLETOWN FARM,** in Newlands offers B & B accomodation suitable for travellers and tourists exploring this fascinating area. The house dates from the 17th century and has recently been carefully renovated to retain its traditional character. Interestingly this farm was featured in Beatrix Potter's 'The Tale of Mrs. Tiggy-Winkle' - *"Once upon a time there was a little girl called Lucie, who lived at a farm called Littletown"*, the story begins.

Today the farm has 8 rooms to let, 6 of which have en-suite bathroom facilities. All of the rooms are light, spacious and well appointed, and enjoy panoramic views. The food, served in the bar/restaurant is excellent, traditional four course farmhouse roasts are available 6 days a week. This is a delightful guesthouse where you will be sure to enjoy your stay.

Littletown Farm, Newlands, Keswick. Tel: 017687 78353

GREYSTOKE, on the B6288, between Caldbeck and Penrith, north of the A66 and Ullswater is another quiet part of Cumbria. It is notable for its magnificent **COLLEGIATE CHURCH** dating from the 13th century, once the home of a college of canons, and as big as a small cathedral. There is a wonderful East Window with much 13th century glass and, in the Lady Chapel, a figure of Madonna and Child carved by a German prisoner-of-war.

About a hundred yards from the church stands **THE PLAGUE STONE** where, during medieval times, coins were left in vinegar in exchange for food for the plague victims. An ancient Sanctuary Stone, now concealed behind a grille, marks the point beyond which fugitives could claim sanctuary.

The village has a fine green, some attractive houses and **GREYSTOKE CASTLE**, now an imposing private house. There are several race-horse stables in the area.

THANET WELL CARAVAN PARK is situated in the beautiful, unspoilt Eden Valley, on the boundaries of the Lake District, mid way between Greystoke and Caldbeck. This small, picturesque park is owned and run by Mary and Collin Dent. There are 60 static and 20 touring pitches in two separate areas; the static pitches, all with fine views of open countryside are either in a lightly wooded area or in a more open aspect. Each site offers the same peace and tranquillity. The area for tourers has all the modern amenities expected by today's touring caravanners including hard roads to all pitches and most with hard standing and electric hook-ups. There is a clean, modern toilet block with showers and a launderette. The site shop and off licence is well stocked and Calor gas and Camping Gaz is available. A perfect, safe place for children the surrounding area has many places of interest all within easy reach.

Thanet Well Caravan Park, Greystoke, Penrith Tel: 01768 484262

HUTTON-IN-THE-FOREST is nearby, and worth visiting is the beautiful historic home of Lord and Lady Inglewood, featuring fine collections of furniture, paintings and tapestries, with a walled garden, topiary terraces and a lovely woodland walk. Hutton-in-the-Forest is about 6 miles to the north west of Penrith, on the B5305 Wigton Road.

NEWTON REIGNY is a few miles south on the River Petteril,

Castlerigg Stone Circle, nr Keswick

north west of Penrith. It takes its name from the de Reigny family who had possessions in this part of Cumbria in the 12th century. The **CHURCH OF ST JOHN**, though restored, dates from the 14th century, and two names carved on a beam near the chancel are reputed to be those of two local carpenters, John Atkenson and Henere Bymert, who constructed a new roof in 1585.

CALTHWAITE. This small village is well worth visiting for here you will find **THE GLOBE INN**, a family run pub which has been in the family for nine years, though Derek and Diana took over the helm two and a half years ago. Set amidst the unspoilt Cumbrian countryside in the peaceful and picturesque village of Calthwaite. It is probably the oldest building in the village and just a couple of miles off the main A6. An ideal setting for a leisurely drive for lunch or Sunday Roast or alternatively, a good base for the touring this lovely area. There are two comfortable letting rooms available all year round and the food is delicious with such tasty dishes as Steak and Ale Pie - a real filler! Good selection of real ales and live entertainment on Saturday night. Find your way here and you will be in good company.

The Globe Inn, Calthwaite, Cumbria.   Tel: 01768 885238

Just south of the A66, heading towards Pooley Bridge and the north east end of Ullswater, is an area of gently undulating countryside where the Lakeland mountains ease into the Eden Valley. Here you will find such charming villages as YANWATH and TIRRIL, both of which have Quaker connections. Yanwath Hall, reputed to be the finest manorial hall in England, was the birthplace of the Quaker Thomas Wilkinson, and in Tirril is an old Quaker Meeting House (now a private house).

Nearby is **DALEMAIN HISTORIC HOUSE AND GARDENS**. Its impressive Georgian facade is just that - it was added on to the Elizabethan house in the eighteenth century. The house itself cannot be said to belong completely to any one era, as it has evolved through a variety of architectural fashions over the centuries. This makes it all the more fascinating to explore; some parts are a confusion of winding stairs and passages, others a series of grand public rooms, housing a rich collection of portraits and fine furniture. Dalemain is surrounded by spectacular gardens with many rare plant species on display.

Barton Old Vicarage

BARTON OLD VICARAGE, owned by Sherie Walker, is tucked away off the Ullswater road between Tirril and Pooley Bridge, 5 minutes drive from it. The large Victorian vicarage stands next to the historically important little medieval church where Wordsworth's grandfather lies buried in the chancel. From this glorious family house, Sherie offers bed and breakfast accommodation, with evening meal if required. The bedrooms are large, with fine views over the large garden towards the mountains of the Lake District. Ullswater, the most beautiful of the larger lakes, is only a short drive away. There is plenty of activity in Pooley Bridge which has three pubs. There are some lovely walks from the house which Sherie is happy to tell you about, she will also arrange bicycles on a loan basis.

Barton Old Vicarage, Barton, Tirril Tel: 01768 486307

POOLEY BRIDGE is a charming Lakeland village within the National Park boundary, at the tip of Ullswater, which many say is the Lake District's most beautiful lake. Its oldest building is part of **HOLLY HOUSE** which dates back to 1691 whilst the 'bridge' of the village's name was begun in 1763. Before Bridge was added, the name Pooley meant 'pool by the hill' and was derived from the pond which existed behind the Sun, and Dunmallard, the cone-shaped hill on the other side of the river.

ULLSWATER it was on the northern shores of Ullswater, at **GLENCOYNE WOOD**, that William Wordsworth, on a bleak and breezy April day, noticed the brilliance of the wild daffodils, an experience that he shared with the world in one of the most quoted poems in the English language; "*I wandered lonely as a cloud....*"

WATERMILLOCK. Just two hundred yards past Watermillock church, on the right, is the small family run- **FAIR PLACE WHOLEFOOD GUESTHOUSE** offering en-suite bedrooms and wholefood and veg-

Lady of the Lake Steamer, Ullswater

etarian breakfasts. From all aspects of the house there are superb open views of the fells with Ullswater a mile below.

Fair Place Wholefood Guesthouse

The building was originally a single storey school built in 1860 and converted by the present owners Dorothy and Ian Bewley in 1957. The en-suite bedrooms have teamakers, colour television and electric fires. A wood burning stove provides warmth in the lounge/dining room on chilly days and for music lovers, there are exceptional facilities for listening, as this is also the Lakeland Home Music's listening room. Breakfast time offers a wide choice including Organic Muesli, cereals, dried and fresh fruits, eggs, tomatoes and mushrooms, 100% wholewheat bread. Children are welcome and pets by arrangement. Please note - There is a 'no smoking' policy.

Seven miles from Junc. 40 on the M6. Follow Ullswater signs A592. When reaching T junction at the Lake, take the right turn, and in exactly one and a half miles at the telephone box, turn right up the hill to find the church, (after one mile), on the left. Fair Place is 200 yds past church on the right).

Fair Place Wholefood Guesthouse, Watermillock-on-Ullswater, Penrith, Cumbria. Tel: 017684 86235.

The **BRACKENRIGG HOTEL** is an 18th century coaching inn overlooking Lake Ullswater just Southwest of Pooley Bridge. Managed by Blanche and Malcolm Tiffin, Brackenrigg Hotel offers all its guests a memorable stay in a beautiful part of the Lake District. The hotel has 11 bedrooms all with either en suite shower or bathroom, along with a family games room, dining room and two bars. Open to non-residents, everyone is welcome to come here and enjoy dinner or a bar meal as well as sample a glass or two of traditional real ale.

Brackenrigg Hotel also offers self-catering accommodation in three tastefully converted cottages situated to the east of the hotel in what were the coaching inn's stables. Each cottage accommodates up to six people and is fully equipped with modern appliances to make your stay as carefree as possible. All self-catering guests are treated as hotel residents with full access to all Brackenrigg's facilities.

Brackenrigg Hotel and Stable Cottages, Watermillock, Lake Ullswater
Tel: 017684 86206

If you are looking for the atmosphere of typical farmhouse accommodation near Penrith, then travel along the A592 (about six miles from Penrith) and aim for Watermillock. Take the road to Watermillock church for half a mile and you will find **LOW LONGTHWAITE FARM** where Margaret Little offers comfortable bed and breakfast accommodation. The cosy 18th century farmhouse has beautiful views over rolling countryside and Ullswater lake. Its an ideal place for family holidays, and the farm environment gives and added interest for children. Take the family pet too. There's home cooking and baking and home made jams for the afternoon tea when you arrive. When phoning to book ask for Margaret.

Farm House Bed & Breakfast, Low Longthwaite, Watermillock, Nr. Penrith.
Tel: 017684 86292

Did You Know...

There is a full

Town and Village Index

at the back of the book?

DACRE is about a mile to the north of Watermillock. The village church in Dacre occupies a site of a former monastery which was mentioned by the Venerable Bede in his accounts of Cumberland in the 8th century. Fragments of masonry are reputed to have come from the monastery and four carvings of bears in the churchyard are probably of Anglo-Viking origin.

DACRE CASTLE is a 14th century pele tower, a type of fortified house or small castle common in Northern England. This was the seat of the Dacre family, Catholic Earls of Cumberland and its turrets and battlements have walls which are eight feet thick. Leonard Dacre took part in the ill-fated 'Rising of the North' in 1589. The estate passed to the Earls of Sussex who restored the castle in 1675 and whose Coat of Arms can still be seen.

Going south from Dacre, between Ullswater and Haweswater, is the Lowther Estate.

ASKHAM, on its edge is a delightful village whose name means 'the place of the ash trees' and it has a large green surrounded by old houses and cottages. From Askham you can look across the River Lowther to the facade of LOWTHER CASTLE; the building is now only a shell, most of it having been demolished in 1957, but it was clearly once a grand place; after one visit Queen Victoria is reputed to have said that she would not return to Lowther Castle as it was too grand for her.

The ancestral owners of the castle were the illustrious Earls of Lonsdale, statesmen and sportsmen. The most famous is perhaps the Fifth Earl (1857-1944), known as the Yellow Earl because of the colour of the livery used on his private carriage. He was the first President of the Automobile Association and permitted his family colours to be used by the Association. The Earl was also a patron of amateur boxing and the Lonsdale Belt emerged from his interest. One of the earlier Lords, better known as Wicked Jimmy, was a famous ghost at the castle. The yellow flag of the Lonsdales can be seen in LOWTHER CHURCH.

There are two Lowther villages, LOWTHER NEWTON, close to the centre of the estate, which was built in the late 17th century to replace an existing village, and LOWTHER, to the east, a remarkable model village designed by the 18th century architect, Robert Adam.

HELTON, south of Askham, is another attractive and secluded village with several interesting 17th and 18th century houses.

Helton, 'town on the side of a hill', is midway between the northern tips of Ullswater and Haweswater, and close by is MOOR DIVOCK, an archaeological site of stone circles and cairns.

BAMPTON-BY-PENRITH is where the road southwards continues to Haweswater. In BAMPTON CHURCH you can see a painting of MARDALE, which was in the village of Mardale, drowned when HAWESWATER, an artificial lake, was constructed and filled as a reservoir to serve the needs of the City of Manchester.

Above Haweswater runs THE HIGH STREET, a Roman road and now one of the most popular fell-walks in the Lake District. It overlooks the remote and lovely BLEA TARN and the lonely valley of MARTINDALE, a cul-de-sac valley south of Ullswater, where England's last remaining herd of wild red deer is often visible from the surrounding fells.

One of the nicest ways to cross from one side of Ullswater to the other is by **LAKE STEAMER**, which links Pooley Bridge with the little village of Glenridding at the opposite end, and at the foot of the Kirkstone Pass. Regular sailings through the summer months allow a boat trip to be combined with a particularly beautiful walk along the eastern shores of Ullswater from Howtown to Sandwick and Patterdale.

Close to the junction of the A592 Glenridding to Penrith road which hugs the shores of Ullswater and the A5091 is the spectacular waterfall, **AIRA FORCE**, now in the ownership of the National Trust. This famous waterfall was the setting for the romantic and tragic story of Emma, who fell in love with a renowned knight called Sir Eglamore. He had to leave her to follow the Crusades. As the months lengthened into years and he had not returned, Emma became so distraught that she started to sleepwalk to Aira Force where she eventually met her tragic death. On his return, the grief-stricken Sir Eglamore became a hermit and lived by the waterfall for the rest of his days.

HARTSOP FOLD, nestling in an unspoilt valley, lies above BROTHERSWATER close to the dramatic Kirkstone Pass. The site has twelve charming lodges to hire for the perfect self-catering holiday. Set in extensive and secluded grounds the Scandinavian lodges have been designed and furnished with guests comfort in mind.

Hartsop Fold

They all have pine fittings and furniture, wall to wall carpets, and well equipped functional kitchens. Sleeping either five or six, pets are welcome be arrangement although four of the lodges are kept pet-free. Once here, there is no need to use a car as there is wonderful scenery just a few yards from the lodge's verandah. The unique situation that Hartsop Fold occupies makes this a holiday destination from which you can discover some of the most picturesque and unspoilt areas of the

National Park. Whether you want an action packed break pursuing a range of outdoor activities or prefer to relax fishing or painting, the life of this secluded, quiet Lakeland area carries on around you as it has done season after season untroubled by the stresses of modern day life.

Hartsop Fold, Banktop House, Lazonby, Penrith Tel: 01768 898268

Leaving Ullswater behind you, continue along the A5091, through MATTERDALE, with its little old church dating from 1573, to the junction with the A66, where a right turn would take you to Penrith and a left turn heads for Keswick, passing through the lovely Lakeland hamlet of SCALES, on the slopes of BLENCATHRA, one of the highest mountains in England.

MUNGRISDALE. **THE OLD VICARAGE** at Mungrisdale is situated 2 miles north of the A66 midway between Keswick and Penrith. The village, nestling at the foot of Souther Fell and Bowscale Fell, is unspoilt, peaceful and tranquil with a pub, Post Office and an internationally recommended restaurant.

The Old Vicarage

The spacious Victorian Vicarage, opposite the church, is full of character and charm. Owned by Pauline and Gordon Bambrough, they offer friendly, family bed and breakfast accommodation is a choice of guest bedrooms. All the rooms have wash hand-basins and tea and coffee facilities and there are two public rooms for guests to use. With a well established, large garden and wonderful views of the Northern Fells

The Moot Hall. Keswick

Cumberland Pencil Museum

this is a perfect place to stay, off the beaten track, in the heart of the Northern Lakes.

The Old Vicarage, Mungrisdale Tel: 01768 779274

PENRUDDOCK. **LOW GARTH** guest house is situated on high ground surrounded by open farmland on the edge of Penruddock village. With Lake Ullswater only 4 miles away, this is an ideal location for exploring the beautiful Lakeland countryside by car, cycle or on foot. Owned by Marion Barritt, Low Garth is a traditional 18th century barn built from local stone which has been sympathetically converted to provide a charming house with magnificent views over the fells. Warm and friendly bed and breakfast accommodation is available in two en suite bedrooms, one of which is suitable for a family. Evening meals are taken, as is the breakfast, in the first floor dining room where the sun can be seen setting over Saddleback with Keswick Valley and Grizedale Pike in the distance. All the meals are freshly prepared from local produce and are just the thing before and after a day touring the Lakes.

Low Garth Guest House, Penruddock, Penrith Tel: 01768 483492

THRELKELD, a little further along the A66 is a village of great charm, famous for its annual **SHEEP DOG TRIALS**. It is the ideal starting point for a number of mountain walks, including an ascent of Blencathra, one of the most exciting of all the Lake District mountains.

THE BUNGALOW, in the village of Threlkeld, makes an ideal centre of walking, climbing, touring or just plain relaxing. Situated on the lower slopes of the Blencathra mountain range there are excellent, unobstructed views over the village towards the Vale of St Johns and the fells around Keswick and Derwentwater. Owned and run by Val and Paul Sunley, there is a choice of self-catering and bed and breakfast accommodation. The Bungalow has five, en suite guest bedrooms all with tea and coffee making facilities and a colour television. Val serves up a hearty, large Lakeland breakfast to fortify you for your day of leisure. Two adjoining bungalows offer self-catering accommodation for up to six adult each. Fully furnished with full fitted kitchen and off peak electric heating you have the benefit of your own place in this delightful spot.

The Bungalow, Sunnyside, Threlkeld Tel: 017687 79679

ST JOHN'S VALE lies between Threlkeld and Keswick. Here you will find **CASTLERIGG**, a remarkable Neolithic circle of 38 stones which commands a superb view of the surrounding fells. Whatever the purpose of the monument, it was a strategic view-point where priests or princes could survey the fell-country.

KESWICK is the largest town within the Lake District Park and its stunning position, surrounded by the mountains of Skiddaw and Borrowdale, and on the shores of Derwent Water, makes it one of Britain's most popular inland holiday resorts.

The volcanic rocks of Borrowdale, newer than the Skiddaw slate group, are rich in minerals, and the discovery of one of the strangest, graphite, led to the development of the pencil industry in Keswick. In the fascinating **CUMBERLAND PENCIL MUSEUM** you can discover the history behind this everyday object, the pencil, through machinery displays and video shows. Children will like the drawing corner with a free drawing competition to enter, as well as the brass rubbing which always proves popular. This unique museum, which follows the story of Cumberland Graphite and the development of the pencil manufacturing industry in Keswick, is of interest to all of us since we have all used these pencils at some time or other. You can pick up a memento of your visit in the Museum Gift Shop which of course sells pencils, in addition to numerous other items.

Cumberland Pencil Museum, Greta Bridge, Keswick 01768 772116

At number 16 Lake Road, Keswick is a most unusual footwear shop of the type rarely to be found anywhere these days. **CARTMELL'S OF KESWICK** is an exclusive shoe shop and has been a speciality foot fitters since 1924. Traditional footwear and truly traditional service has always been at the forefront of this business and since Mrs Askew, the proprietor, took over the business in 1972, she has been responsible for the expansion in size of the premises which now has a forty foot frontage in beautiful English Oak, Fine footwear from exclusive manufacturers such as Crockett & Jones, Barkers, Carcavelos, Sioux, Amalfi, Church, and many more are a feature of Cartmells. Mrs Audrey Askew was born and bred in the fitting trade and was trained in her father's shop - Thomas Walker (Est. 1814) in Huddersfield. It was sold to Church in 1969, and with her father, she acquired Cartmell's in 1972. Apart from her considerable knowledge and a lifetime of dedication to the footwear trade, the real secret of this business is the quality stock, an incredible range of fitting widths and sizes, and a mail order service second to none. For the ladies - sizes 2-11 with fittings AA to F; and for the Gentlemen sizes 5-13 with fittings C to H. Mrs. Askew and her staff give special personal attention to correct measuring to ensure footwear fits perfectly - catering also for those with special orthopaedic needs. For those unable to call at the shop, there is a mail order service, and by supplying specific measurements and a pattern of the foot, Cartmell's can then send your order to you with a promise to exchange or refund if they should prove unsuitable. The many customer testimonials prove the success of this area of the business. Since it is becoming increasingly difficult to get good quality well fitting narrow width shoes, a number of American manufactures are breaking into the U.K. market with new and younger styles and Cartmell's are including the best from such ranges in their selection. Mrs Askew has always been particular to ensure the finest stock of good looking, well made, comfortable leather shoes are available at Cartmell's.

Cartmell's of Keswick Ltd., 16 Lake Road, Keswick, Cumbria.
Tel: 017687 72740

Keswick offers many opportunities to the traveller and tourist. Apart from the wonderful lakeland countryside, the town itself has many interesting shops and businesses; one of which is **FOCUS OF LAKELAND** in 43 Main Street. Colin and Amanda Waite have established their family business here over seven years, during which time they have won national recognition for their quality work. They are both photographers, and their portrait studio offers an ideal opportunity for family portraits while visitors are on holiday and in a relaxed frame of mind. They are ideally placed to take photographs of the local area which they sell on the premises together with prints taken from old 'glass' negatives which they have collected over the years. Focus of Lakeland are also stockists of Lakeland Contemporary Art and Victorian prints. Additionally, their one hour photographic developing and printing service makes this an essential place to visit, and if time is very limited, they even offer a mail order service.

Focus of Lakeland, 43 Main Street, Keswick, Cumbria. Tel: 017687 74572

On Keswick's Main Street, close to the Moot Hall, you will find **BRYSON'S BAKERY AND CAFE**. Brysons began baking bread and cakes fifty years ago at the shop and bakery in Maud Street.

Bryson's Bakery and Cafe

Since these early beginnings the business has grown to have an enviable reputation for the high quality of its bread and cakes. Particularly noteworthy, and well worth sampling, are its Fruit Cake and Lakeland Plum Bread, both of which have a reputation which extends throughout the country. All of its products are freshly baked at the shop and they can be enjoyed at the tearoom which has a very friendly atmosphere and top quality service.

Bryson's Bakery and Cafe, 38/42 Main Street, Keswick. Tel: 017687 72257

For those wishing to make Keswick the centre for their stay in this area of the Lake District, **BIRCH HOW** offers a central location in the town and is closely situated to Fitz Park and the Leisure Pool while being within easy reach of Derwentwater, the Borrowdale Valley and many other beauty areas. This small guest house has three letting bedrooms all of which have colour television and tea & coffee making facilities. Evening meals can be provided as well as packed lunches. Special diets are catered for and children are welcome.

Birch How, 41 Brunholme Terrace, Station Road, Keswick.
Tel: 017687 73404

You can be sure of an enjoyable and relaxing stay at the Georgian style **ACORN HOUSE HOTEL** in Keswick.

Acorn House Hotel

The proprietors, Joe and Susan Miller, pride themselves on the warm and friendly atmosphere. The 10 spacious and luxurious guest rooms are traditionally furnished and individually designed. All have en-suite facilities, central-heating colour televisions, radio alarms, tea and coffee making facilities and hospitality trays. Three of the rooms have beautiful four-poster beds and are ideal for romantic occasions. A generous full English breakfast will set you up for the day, whether walking, climbing or sightseeing. After the day's exertions you can relax in the elegant and comfortable lounge, or enjoy the attractive and well-tended gardens. Situated on Ambleside Road, close to the centre of the town.

Acorn House Hotel, Ambleside Road, Keswick. Tel: 017687 72553

Set in 40 acres of glorious gardens and woodland next to the B5289 road to Borrowdale, **THE STAKIS KESWICK LODORE HOTEL** overlooks Derwentwater and is ideally located close to all of the Lake District's most interesting attractions and activities.

The Stakis Keswick Lodore Hotel

This has to be one of the very best hotels in the area, it is magnificently equipped with fine facilities which include a newly finished leisure club with a superb indoor swimming pool, sauna, solarium, a heated outdoor swimming pool, a games room, tennis court, squash court, games room, hairdresser, beauty salon and a children's nursery with fully qualified NNEB registered nannies. The nursery is open daily from 8am. to 6pm.for children under the age of six, baby sitting and baby listening can be easily arranged. The hotel has an enviable reputation for its excellent local and international cuisine. The 70 bedrooms are accessible by lift, have en-suite bathrooms and are individually decorated and superbly equipped. Guests are entitled to free admission to Keswick Golf Club (mid-week only), the Cumberland Pencil Museum or The World of Beatrix Potter in Bowness.

Situated in beautiful gardens just 100 metres from the hotel, **LODORE HOUSE** is a luxury five bedroom bungalow available for self catering holidays. The house is centrally heated, has a fully equipped kitchen, real log fires and spacious rooms, indeed it has everything that

Friar's Crag

you could possibly require. The views across Derwentwater are superb, this is a truly idyllic setting for the perfect self-catering holiday.

Stakis Keswick Lodore Hotel, Keswick, Cumbria. Tel: 017687 77285

A short walk out of the town centre, along the Lake Road and past the bustling lakeside promenade, will take you to the popular **CENTURY THEATRE** and **FRIAR'S CRAG**. This famous view of the Derwent Water and its islands, now National Trust property, formed one of John Ruskin's early childhood memories.

PORTINSCALE. **DERWENT COTTAGE**, a large 18th century Lakeland house, is situated in an acre of beautiful, mature gardens in the quiet village of Portinscale near Keswick and Derwentwater. The house enjoys splendid views across the valley to Skiddaw and has five well equipped and spacious bedrooms, all individually furnished and decorated and complete with en-suite bathroom facilities. The light, airy dining room is meticulously kept, each table is laid with crisp linen, gleaming silver cutlery and sparkling crystal ware. The fresh, home cooked food is delightful, full English breakfast is served between 8:30 and 9:00am., in the evening the four-course candle-lit table d'hote meal is served and can be accompanied with a fine wine from the extensive wine list. A no-smoking establishment, children over 12 are welcome, pets are not.

Derwent Cottage, Portinscale, Keswick, Cumbria. Tel: 017687 74838

Although the centre of Keswick is busy, it has quieter places. Just behind the central shopping area is a little park alongside the River Greta. Not far away the fascinating **FITZ PARK MUSEUM AND ART GALLERY** has an unusual stone xylophone and an important collection of manuscripts by Wordsworth and Southey.

Keswick also has a close association with **THE NATIONAL TRUST**. Canon Rawnsley, the local vicar, was one of the founder members of the Trust, which he helped to set up in 1895. Rawnsley fought for years to get **BRANDLEHOW WOODS AND FELL** for the Trust, raising £7000 in five months. This was the first National Trust property in the Lake

District, and it has grown since then to include most of the Central Fell area. However, despite the help of Rawnsley's contemporaries such as William Morris, John Ruskin and Thomas Carlyle, he couldn't prevent Manchester Corporation from flooding the two natural lakes of THIRLMERE, which submerged the old road and hamlets of ARMBOTH and WYTHBURN, and the bridge which had joined the two lakes where Wordsworth and Coleridge used to meet each other. WYTHBURN CHURCH survives, a favourite spot from which to start the climb up HELVELLYN.

THIRLSPOT is nearby, at the foot of Helvellyn on the A591 Grasmere to Keswick road.

BRAITHWAITE may be reached by leaving Keswick heading west on the A66, towards Cockermouth. On the way, visit LINGHOLM, home of Lord and Lady Rochdale. It has very impressive gardens and woodland, open to the public through the summer, and great views. Beatrix Potter's family used Lingholm for many years as a holiday home and it crops up in many of the writer's tales. The woods here were SQUIRREL NUTKIN'S HOME. Just north, at FAWE PARK, is BENJAMIN BUNNY COUNTRY, and to the south, at NEWLANDS VALLEY, Mrs Tiggy Winkle lived up the side of CAT BELLS.

Lyzzick Hall

Nearby Lyzzick Hall was originally the country residence of a successful 19th century textile merchant. The name 'Lyzzick' dates back to Medieval times and means 'light oak'. Today the LYZZICK HALL HOTEL, situated in spacious, rambling gardens on the lower slopes of Skiddaw, offers exceptional standards of accomodation, hospitality and comfort. The views of the Derwentwater Fells across the valley are astounding and are best enjoyed from the sunny dining room whilst selecting a meal from the extensive menus. The chef is one of the best in the area and his wide experience certainly shows, the cuisine is exquisite. This luxuriously appointed hotel boasts its own outdoor heated swimming pool and two comfortable lounges stocked with games and pastimes, one specifically for non-smokers. The twenty-five bedrooms all have en-suite bathrooms and are equipped with colour television, radio and telephone. Alfredo and Dorothy Fernandez are understandably very proud of the fine reputation that their hotel enjoys and you can be sure that the warmest of welcomes will be extended to you during your stay whatever the time of year. Situated on the A591between the Northern tip of Derwentwater and the Southern tip of Bassenthwaite. AA/RAC 2 Star, ETB 4 Crowns Highly Commended.

Lyzzick Hall Hotel, Underskiddaw, Keswick-on-Derwentwater.
Tel: 017687 72277

Overlooking the slopes of Skiddaw, and set against Thornthwaite Forest , **GALLERY MEWS COTTAGES**, tucked away in the village of THORNTHWAITEoff the A66, offer spacious self contained self-catering accommodation ideal for families touring this area. Each cottage is superbly appointed and completely equipped and you will be sure to enjoy a stay here.

Additionally, Thornthwaite Galleries, set in a charming, warm old building houses some of the most splendid examples of artistic skill, craftsmanship and unusual items that you are likely to find anywhere in the National Park.

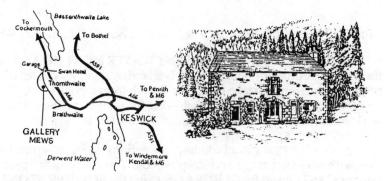

Gallery Mews Cottages, Randlehow, Mockerkin, Cockermouth. Cumbria.
Tel: 01946 861018

DUBWATH, another lovely hamlet nestles in this beautiful, un-spoilt area around **BASSENTHWAITE LAKE**.

As you near the end of Bassenthwaite Lake you will enter a delightful section of wooded dual carriageway. As this section ends look for the road sign to 'Castle Inn', a right turn Following the signs to the inn will take you across Ouse Bridge at the head of the lake. In a few hundred yards you will see a breathtaking sight to your right as you look down the entire length of the lake. A few moments later you will see a splendid hotel on the left hand side, **THE CASTLE INN HOTEL**. This hotel is set in its own grounds, just a few minutes walk from the lake and enjoys fine views towards Borrowdale. The restaurant 'Le Chateau' is well known for the quality of its food and the efficient, friendly service. You can savour the delights of meals prepared with the finest ingredients, presented with style and an eye for detail. All of the bedrooms have an en-suite bathroom, colour television, tea and coffee-making facilities, radio and direct-dial telephone. The deluxe rooms are exceptionally spacious and have a separate lounge area. The hotel also has extensive leisure facilities which include a tennis court, a large indoor swimming pool, saunas, solarium, fitness room, snooker, badminton and table tennis. Fishing and shooting can be easily arranged, as can a free mid-week round of golf.

The Castle Inn Hotel, Bassenthwaite Lake, Nr Keswick. Tel: 017687 76401

At the southern end of **DERWENT WATER** is **CAT BELLS**, one of the most beautiful ridge-walks in all England. A good way to set off for such an excursion is to take the motor-launch from Keswick to **HAWSE END**, where the ascent begins. Following the path along the ridge, you will descend again to the ancient hamlet of **GRANGE IN BORROWDALE**.

BORROWDALE is a brooding, mysterious valley, steep and narrow with towering crags and deep woods. You can wander past the famous **CASTLE** and **EAGLE CRAGS**, climb the **BOWDER STONE** or, best of all, take a choice of paths through the thickly-wooded hillside over to the hamlet of **ROSTHWAITE**, in the centre of Borrowdale.

Here you will find **ROSE COTTAGE**, which provides two comfortable flats, each for two people, above the only **GENERAL STORES** in the valley. Geoff and Pam Truckle are justly proud of the fine reputation for high standards that their shop and self catering accomodation enjoys.

The shop stocks an incredibly wide range of provisions (bread, frozen foods, fresh milk and groceries etc.) and it is open daily throughout the year apart from Christmas Day. In addition to food the store supplies newspapers, some outdoor wear and equipment, and also carries an 'off-sales licence'.

The flats are self-contained and each has its own staircase leading from the entrance. Both are centrally heated, comfortably furnished, and carpeted throughout and include an electric cooker, fridge, toaster, crockery, cutlery, cooking utensils, iron and ironing board and Colour TV. An ideal place to 'get away from it all' or to stock up for your journey.

Rose Cottage and General Store, Rosthwaite, Nr Keswick. Tel: 017687 77678

On an elevated site in the heart of Borrowdale, **GREENBANK**, a lovely Victorian house, enjoys magnificent views of the valley and Derwentwater. Here is the perfect, peaceful base for a break spent fell walking, climbing or simply touring the Lake District.

Greenbank

The rooms in the house are spacious and comfortable. There are two lounges, both with log fires, one with a TV. The ten bedrooms are all attractively decorated and well equipped, all have en-suite bath or shower and toilet facilities. Some enjoy a view of the lake. On arrival guests are welcomed with a tray of tea; a superb, home cooked four course evening meal and full English breakfast is also provided. ETB 3 Crowns Highly Commended.

Greenbank, Borrowdale, Cumbria. Tel: 017687 77215

The view from Ashness towards Keswick, across Derwent Water, with the little hump-backed bridge in the foreground, is one of the most photographed in England.

A couple of miles along the valley, at the bottom of **HONISTER HAUSE**, the pass which leads over to Buttermere, is SEATOLLER. From here begins the famous and well-trodden track, via **SEATHWAITE**, over **STYHEAD PASS** to **SCAFELL PIKE**, England's highest mountain.

The regular bus service between Seathwaite and Keswick describes itself, with some justification, as the most beautiful bus ride in Britain. It certainly is lovely and gives access to the whole of Borrowdale.

CHAPTER SIX

South Lakeland

Kentmere Hall

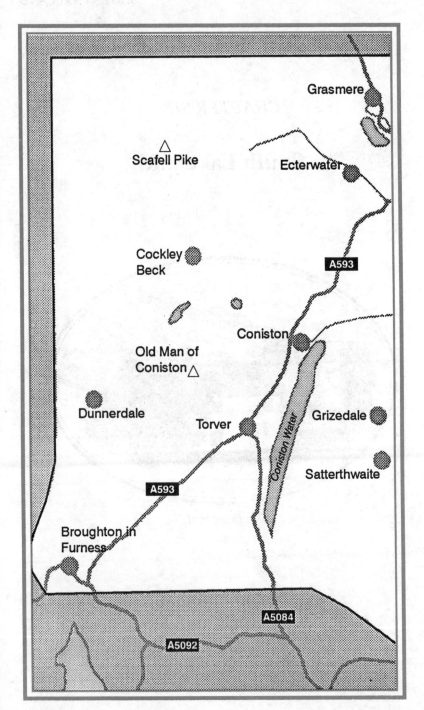

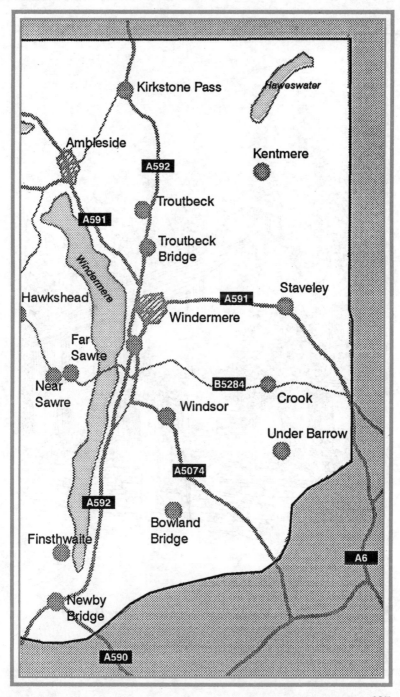

Kirkstone Pass

Haweswater

Ambleside

Kentmere

A592

Troutbeck

A591

Troutbeck
Bridge

Windermere

Staveley

A591

Hawkshead

Windermere

Far
Sawre

Near
Sawre

B5284

Crook

Windsor

Under Barrow

A5074

A592

A6

Finsthwaite

Bowland
Bridge

Newby
Bridge

A590

Dove Cottage, Wordsworth's Grasmere Home

CHAPTER SIX

South Lakeland

The southern part of the Lake District is Cumbria's best known and most popular area, with the main resort towns of Windermere and Bowness, and the picturesque villages with all their literary associations. The great English poet, William Wordsworth, spent all his life in this area and loved to walk for miles through the countryside, with Helvellyn in the background, drawing inspiration for some of his greatest work from his surroundings.

Coleridge, De Quincey, Southey and Ruskin also spent much of their lives around the lakes of Grasmere, Windermere and Coniston. Beatrix Potter, creator of Peter Rabbit, Squirrel Nutkin and other famous characters, lived at Sawrey, and Arthur Ransome based all of his Swallows and Amazons books around Coniston. The list goes on, and it is easy to understand how the landscape has inspired such creativity in these and so many other writers and artists.

The focal point of Wordsworth Country is the picturesque village of Grasmere, in its particularly lovely mountain setting, close to its very pretty lake of the same name and with craggy hills all around.

GRASMERE is a small village and gets extremely busy, but it is delightful to walk around and worth braving the crowds before you head for the more hidden places of South Lakeland.

One road winds its way through the village, past **ST OSWALD'S CHURCH**, where William Wordsworth and many members of his family are buried in the churchyard.

Barney's News Box and Call of the Wild

Along Broadgate in Grasmere you'll find **BARNEY'S NEWS BOX** specialising in Jigsaw puzzles from 300 pieces to 8000 pieces - just the thing for a gift or a rainy spell in the Lakes. With a stock of over four thousand items you should have no difficulty finding those presents to take home, or you could have them dispatched by the mail order service available.

Next door to Barneys is **THE CALL OF THE WILD,** a shop where all the gifts have a 'Wildlife' theme. A donation is given to charity from every purchase you make. Good gifts with a good cause!

Barneys News Box & Call of the Wild, Broadgate, Grasmere, Cumbria.
Tel: 015394 35627

Lovers of Lakeland art will find a veritable haven at **THE HEATON COOPER STUDIO.** It houses a permanent exhibition of work by W. Heaton Cooper R.I. (1903 - 1995) and his father, A Heaton Cooper (1863 - 1929), both of whom are recognised as the foremost artists of the area. It is a real family business, with Julian Cooper, the grandson of Alfred Heaton Cooper, and son of renowned sculptress, Ophelia Gordon Bell, inheriting the artistic talent. The family now offer the largest collection of Lakeland prints and greeting cards in the area which has been built up over the last fifty years. There are various Ophelia Gordon Bell sculptures on show as well as a comprehensive range of artist materials from the basic to the unusual, with drawing and water colour papers a speciality.

The Heaton Cooper Studios, Grasmere, Cumbria.
Tel: 015394 35280 Fax: 015394 35797

No trip to Grasmere is complete, of course, without a visit to the **WORDSWORTH MUSEUM** and **DOVE COTTAGE,** where William and his sister Dorothy lived from 1799 - 1808. In 1802 William married Mary and she came to join the Dove Cottage household. Coleridge and De Quincey often came to stay - in fact, one gets the impression that they came perhaps just a little too often, indulging in quantities of opium and swelling numbers uncomfortably in this rather small house, where newspaper lined the walls for warmth and economy, and for much of their time here, the Wordsworths could afford little more to eat than porridge. This must have been an eccentric household, and the guided tour of Dove Cottage paints a very clear picture of their lifestyle, with a little insight into the unusual relationship between Dorothy, William and Mary Wordsworth. In the museum, the Wordsworth Trust's collection is inspiringly presented, and includes original Wordsworth manuscripts, letters exchanged between Wordsworth and his friends, and extracts from the original of Dorothy's journals. Give yourself half a day to visit this and Dove Cottage.

Where to eat? So often the question by the visiting tourist or businessman. If you are spending an evening in the ever popular village of Grasmere then seek out **LE LAC RESTAURANT**; it's set back off Red Lion Square in Langdale Road and away from the hubbub of the busy village. There you will find Derek and Muriel Lack, the proprietors, who will welcome you to this busy French and Vegetarian restaurant which open seven days a week in the evenings. There is a varied and most interesting menu and, as you might expect, fresh and seasonal food is used whenever possible. Children can be accommodated and help is available for disabled clients. Very pleasant and busy atmosphere. Good parking opposite the restaurant.

Le Lac Restaurant, Langdale Road, Grasmere, Cumbria. Tel: 015394 35039

Grasmere is a good central point to explore both north and south Lakeland, and there are some fine walks from here into **EASEDALE**, over to **GRIZEDALE** and **PATTERDALE**, or over **GREENUP EDGE** into Borrowdale. Once you have walked out of the village and begin to climb out of the valley, you will be away from the congestion, instead rewarded by the most breathtaking views across the lake of Grasmere and its neighbour, RYDAL WATER.

If you are staying around Grasmere, but prefer somewhere a step away from the busy village, there are numerous hotels and bed & breakfast places nearby, from which you can get out to the fells easily, or in to explore more of Grasmere itself.

Enjoying an enviable location about half a mile from Grasmere village, overlooking the tranquil scenery of Easedale, **LANCRIGG VEGETARIAN COUNTRY HOUSE HOTEL** offers you everything you could possibly want for that quiet break away from it all.

Lancrigg Vegetarian Country House Hotel

Once a favourite haunt of Wordsworth, Lancrigg was bought by his friend Elizabeth Fletcher in 1839 and soon became a meeting place for Lakeland poets. Today it provides luxurious accommodation in individually styled guest rooms. A mouthwatering wholesome menu is enjoyed in elegant, candlelit surroundings to a backdrop of soothing classical music. With 30 acres of woodland gardens to explore, leading to spectacular views of the nearby fells, you may well end your stay at Lancrigg feeling you have had a taste of heaven! Winner of the award for the 'Vegetarian Hotel of the Year' in the North West region, this hotel comes highly recommended.

Lancrigg Vegetarian Country House Hotel, Easedale, Grasmere
Tel: 01539 435317

Lake View Country Guest House

Just 100 yards off the centre of the popular village of Grasmere is **LAKE VIEW COUNTRY GUEST HOUSE** owned by Peter and Beth Mosey. Formerly a farmhouse built around the mid 1800's, it is set in

132

three quarters of an acre of the most beautiful scenic countryside overlooking the lake with a private path leading to it.

There are six letting rooms some of which are on suite. Peter and Beth also have three self-catering apartments which are let weekly in the main season but are available for daily lets in the off season. Evening meals are available with prior notice. An ideal location.

Lake View Country House, Grasmere, Cumbria. Tel: 015394 35384.

Just a little way outside Grasmere the Wordsworth story continues at **RYDAL MOUNT**, where William, his sister and his wife lived from 1813 until 1850, when he died. This is a handsome house, overlooking Rydal Water, and it is still owned by descendants of the Wordsworth family, who have opened it to the public, as well as the gardens that William laid out himself. Among other possessions on display, the house contains the only portrait of Wordsworth's sister, Dorothy. From the Grasmere end of Rydal Water there are some lovely walks around the two lakes or to the summit of **LOUGHRIGG FELL**, an easily manageable walk which rewards with breathtaking views of the lakes.

AMBLESIDE, south of Grasmere on the A591, also a centre for extremely good walks, most notably into the high fells to the north of the town.

In the very heart of the Lake District, yet close to the centre of Ambleside and Lake Windermere, is the **ROTHAY MANOR HOTEL**. The Manor, once the home of a prosperous Liverpool merchant, is built in the Regency style and retains many of the original features including carved acanthus leafed corners and an imposing first floor veranda with cast iron railings. Not surprisingly this is a listed building.

Rothay Manor Hotel

Opened in 1967, this is a family run hotel and restaurant that is renowned for its high standard of service. All the hotel's fifteen bedrooms have en suite bathrooms and each is individually designed and furnished in a comfortable and gracious style. For extra privacy and space there are three luxury suites available in the grounds of the hotel.

As well as offering efficient personal service which makes every guest feel truly at ease the hotel restaurant is an experience to be savoured. The menu is varied and each dish is prepared with flair and imagination. The personally compiled wine list, covering all the wine regions of the world, ensures that each diner has the perfect accompaniment to any meal. The spacious and classical dining room, with its relaxed atmosphere and views of the gardens, is the perfect setting for any occasion.

Rothay Manor, Rothay Bridge, Ambleside Tel: 015394 33605

Ambleside is a pretty town - look out for the **OLD BRIDGE HOUSE**, a tiny cottage perched on a little packhorse bridge in the centre of the town, now a National Trust shop. In the 1850's this was the home of Mr and Mrs Rigg and their six children - the main room of this one-up, one-down house measures 13ft x 6ft!

Every effort is made by the Haywood family to ensure your time at **ELDER GROVE HOTEL**, Ambleside, is relaxing and thoroughly enjoyable. There is a choice of twelve beautifully furnished, centrally heated bedrooms, all with private bathrooms and many with delightful views over the surrounding fells. The rooms are fully equipped with all luxuries. The day starts with a traditional full Cumbrian breakfast and in the evening a beautifully prepared dinner awaits in the soft glow of candlelight. A glance at the Visitor's Book will confirm the satisfaction enjoyed by visitors from many parts of the world. Located close to the centre of Ambleside giving easy access to all areas of the Lakes. ETB 3-Crown Commended, RAC Highly Commended and AA 2 star.

Elder Grove Hotel, Lake Road, Ambleside, Cumbria. Tel: 015394 32504.

A steep road climbs sharply out of the town centre, from the A591 Keswick - Windermere road, known locally as **THE STRUGGLE**, up to the dramatic **KIRKSTONE PASS**, and over to Ullswater, making this a convenient position from which to explore the whole of the Lake District.
The **KIRKSTONE PASS INN** in now popular with walkers and

The Old Bridge House, Ambleside

skiers who call in to warm themselves with hot chocolate or mulled wine. The inn's original character is evident in the bar's low ceilings, oak beams and open log fires, and upstairs the comfortable guest rooms come complete with four-poster beds and beautiful quilts. There is a variety of wholesome home-cooked food available, one of the favourites being Corned Beef and Leek Pie. All these factors combine to ensure an unforgettable experience for all who stay here, the third highest pub in England at 15000 feet.

The Kirkstone Pass is so called because of a stone at the top which looks like a church steeple when approached from the North, and Kirk is still used in Scotland today as their word for 'church'.

Kirkstone Pass Inn, Kirkstone Pass, Ambleside, Cumbria. Tel: 015394 33624

From the centre of Ambleside, follow the A591 south towards the town of Windermere, skirting the edge of LAKE WINDERMERE. This is a very pretty drive at any time of the year, along a tree-lined stretch of the lake which changes colour dramatically with each season.

TOWN END, built in about 1626 by a yeoman farmer called George Browne, was occupied by the Browne family until 1944. The house is now open to the public and contains a collection of the family's furniture, tools and artefacts over the generations.

TROUTBECK, next to TROUTBECK BRIDGE, is well worth a visit. With views of Windermere to the foot of the valley and those of Coniston and Grasmere only slightly further distant, the MORTAL MAN HOTEL at Troutbeck is ideally placed for appreciation of the Lakeland and its views. Other landmarks in view are Wasswater and its parent peaks - Scafell and Great Gable. The name of the Inn (Est. 1689) is derived from a famous old sign painted by Julius Caesar Ibbetson who died in 1817. The Inn attracts many visitors on its own merits which almost outweigh those of its glorious situation. There are twelve bedrooms with fine views around Troutbeck valley each with radio, television telephone and trouser press. The en-suite facilities for all the bedrooms include bath, shower and hairdryer. In the restaurant the table d'hôte menu offers imaginative dishes prepared with fresh produce accompanied by a well chosen wine list. The bar adjacent to the Resident's Lounge offers an intimate and warm atmosphere where a light lunch may also be enjoyed.

The Mortal Man, Troutbeck, Windermere, Cumbria.
Tel: 015394 33193. Fax: 015394 31261

WINDERMERE is perhaps the Lake District's best known tourist centre. The confusion of names between the town and the lake goes back to the days when the Kendal and Windermere Railway Company was opened in 1847. Its terminal station was at the village of Birthwaite - hardly a name to bring the tourists flocking in - so the railway company called their station Windermere, even though it is over a mile away from the lake. In the early days carriages and , in later years, buses linked the station with the landing stages in the village of Bowness on the shores of the lake.

Such was the popularity of the Lake District, even in Victorian times, that a town filled with hotels, boarding houses, comfortable villas and shops soon sprang up around the railway station. It spread rapidly down the hill towards the lake until Bowness and Birthwaite were linked together under the name of Windermere Town, the lake being given the unnecessary prefix, 'Lake' Windermere.

Windermere's railway line remains open as a single track branch - 'The Lakes Line' - now the only surviving British Rail line to run into the heart of the Lake District. Modern diesel railcars provide a busy shuttle service to and from the express services at Oxenholme. The rail journey via Kendal, Burneside and Staveley is a delight, and a very pleasant alternative to the crowded A591 road.

Within a few yards of Windermere Station, just across the busy main road, there is a footpath that leads through the woods to one of the finest viewpoints in Lakeland, **ORREST HEAD**. It takes about an hour from the station to climb and descend the little hillock but there is no better introduction to this part of Cumbria.

ROCKSIDE GUEST HOUSE, is an attractive traditional stone and slate built house. Close to the station and with its own off-road parking, Rockside offers excellent accommodation in a house full of character and charm. There are fifteen guest rooms ranging from single to family rooms, most with en-suite shower room and all with colour TV, radio, clock, telephone and central heating. With Windermere lake less than a mile away, and a tempting array of shops, restaurants and pubs in the village centre, Rockside makes an ideal base from which to explore this beautiful area of the Lake District.

Rockside Guest House, Ambleside Road, Windermere, Cumbria.
Tel: 015394 45343

Just a few minutes away from the centre of Windermere, and not far from the lake shore, is the peaceful and tranquil haven that is **BIRTHWAITE EDGE**. Originally the house was the rectory for the Rev Miles Moss who was, at one time, the Vicar of Windermere.

Birthwaite Edge

Now tastefully converted and extended this residence offers ten fully equipped self catering apartments, each individually styled and furnished, to accommodate from two to six people. There are fine views, from all the apartments, of the well established gardens and beyond to the glorious countryside of pikes and fells. Birthwaite Edge has its own

138

private open air swimming pool and all that Windermere and the lake have to offer is close by. Personally supervised and maintained by Bruce and Marsha Dodsworth, the units make a perfect base for any family holiday.

Birthwaite Edge, Birthwaite Road, Windermere Tel: 015394 42861

Just a little way out of the town centre, a visit to **BROCKHOLE NATIONAL PARK CENTRE** is one of the best ways to begin exploring. This Edwardian country house and estate has been carefully transformed into a visitor centre with displays and exhibitions of the Lake District National Park, its wildlife and customs. There is a restaurant and an excellent bookshop, but above all, miles of woodland and lakeside paths to explore, never more lovely than in the spring when the wild daffodils grow prolifically between the trees.

Call into Windermere's **TOURIST INFORMATION CENTRE** too, which is full of useful maps, guide books and information about all the local attractions.

MEREWOOD COUNTRY HOUSE HOTEL, at Ecclerigg, is an impressive establishment standing in 20 acres of landscaped woodland gardens, overlooking Lake Windermere. Here the warm welcome is matched by the comfort and luxury of the sumptuous surroundings. The Conservatory Bar is evocative of the Edwardian era, with its mahogany panelling, beautiful mosaic floor and red chesterfield sofas. In the Billiard Room Restaurant with its elegant yew tables, you can enjoy a first class menu of English and French cuisine, including a creative range of vegetarian dishes all accompanied by an extensive international wine list. Upstairs equal thought and care has gone into the individually decorated bedrooms. All very spacious, beautifully furnished and with the top class facilities you would expect. It therefore comes as no surprise to learn that Merewood has received the five crown, highly commended award, one of the English Tourist Board's highest accolades. Having stayed here recently, we think it is ideal for a spoil yourself weekend. They do a very good dinner, bed and breakfast; recommended.

Merewood Country House Hotel, Ecclerigg, Windermere Tel: 015394 46484

CRAGWOOD COUNTRY HOUSE HOTEL is situated idyllically in acres of secluded gardens and woodland with magnificent views of the Old Man of Coniston, Scafell, Fairfield and Langdale Pikes and Lake Windermere. The House was designed by Frank Dunkley and built in 1910 for the industrialist Albert Warburton and featured in a 1912 edition of Country Life where it was noted for 'the well modelled plaster work that adorns the beams of the reception rooms'; a feature that remains to this day. The traditional wood panelled hall leads into a bar and two exceedingly comfortable lounges, light and airy in the summer and cosy and warmed by log fires in the winter. There are two dining rooms which both offer the best in imaginative country house cuisine. The original and varied menus are based on local fresh produce, enhanced by herbs from the hotels own garden and complimented by an extensive wine list. The 23 bedrooms all offer the latest in modern comfort in charmingly decorated settings. All are en suite except one bedroom which has a private bathroom opposite. The Edwardian gardens were landscaped at the turn of the century and the grounds lead down to the shore of Windermere lake where the hotel has half a mile of lake frontage. A truly charming hotel which has retained the elegance of the Edwardian era.

Please Don't Forget...

To tell people that you read about them in

The Hidden Places

Cragwood Country House Hotel, Windermere Tel: 015394 88177

Walkers finishing the 81 mile Dales Way Walk from Ilkley to Bowness have their first sight of Lake Windemere from the slopes of Brantfell, one of the small hills overlooking Bowness village. From its modest summit there are magnificent views of Lake Windemere, the Lakeland Hills, the Pennines and Morecambe Bay. On the road leading up to Brantfell, you will find the Fairfield Country House Hotel and Spinnery Cottage self catering apartments, both owned and managed by Ray and Barbara Hood. The properties achieved fame in the early part of the century whilst they were occupied by Annie Garnett, the famous water colourist, gardener, designer, and manufacturer of fabrics and textiles. Her three acres of garden provided the inspiration for much of her work with many of her floral designs being transferred to handwoven fabrics. The secluded garden, now much smaller than when it was so lovingly created by Annie Garnett, is still a centre of attraction, and Ray and Barbara are justly proud of the camelia, azalea, rhododendron and the magnificent wisteria that is probably as old as the house itself. The premises, which were built by Annie's grandfather around 1800 are now the Fairfield Hotel where all nine bedrooms have private bath or shower rooms, colour televisions, tea and coffee making facilities etc. All have been recently refurbished and redecorated. The lounge boasts a roaring log fire for those chilly evenings and the hotel is centrally heated throughout. Breakfasts here are an English feast. This is the peaceful setting for the warm and friendly atmosphere that awaits visitors to the Fairfield Hotel. Annie Garnett converted the stables of the old house into a working spinnery and in the early part of the century the buildings were extended to provide space for 8 looms. This is now Spinnery Cottage which has been tastefully converted into 4 self-catering flats, each having a separate bedroom, bath or shower room, lounge and kitchen area; one of the flats has a second bedroom with two bunk beds. The flats are available throughout the year and short lets can be booked during the low season.

Fairfield Country House Hotel and Spinnery Cottage self-catering apartments, Brantfell Road, Bowness, Cumbria.
Tel:015394 46565 or 015394 44884

BOWNESS is an attractive, albeit busy, town, right on the edge of the lake, and it is from here that most of the lake cruises operate.

For those looking to expend a little energy during their holidays, a visit to **WINDERMERE CYCLES** on South Terrace in Bowness could provide an enjoyable and worthwhile experience. David Ashton started selling cycles in 1983 and now, as well as the sale of bikes, has built a very successful business hiring out Mountain Bikes, Tandems and all kinds of cycles for adults and children. Rates are very flexible from half-day to weekly with special family concessions. David also provides guided day or evening tours during the summer months with packed lunches if required, or you could even book a weekend holiday package with guide, mechanic, cycling, bed and breakfast and evening meals all included. Seems a great idea!

Windermere Cycles, South Terrace, Bowness, Cumbria.
Tel: 015394 44479 & 47779

More than just England's largest lake, Windermere is actually a public highway or, more correctly, waterway. This ten-mile stretch of water, with its thickly wooded banks and scattered islands, has been used since Roman times as a means of transport. Roman Legionnaires used it for carrying stone to their fort at 'Galava', near present-day Ambleside, at the head of the lake. The monks of Furness Abbey fished for pike and char - a rare form of trout and a local delicacy. When the railway came, handsome paddle-steamers linked Bowness with Ambleside and LAKESIDE at the southern end of the lake where the Railway Company had a station and an hotel. The hotel and station survive, as does the railway as far as the village of HAVERTHWAITE. It is operated, during the summer months, by the **LAKESIDE AND HAVERTHWAITE STEAM RAILWAY COMPANY.**

There are few nicer ways to spend a summer day in the Lake District than taking one of the handsome, vintage boats of the **WINDERMERE IRON STEAMBOAT COMPANY** from Ambleside or Bowness Pier down to Lakeside for a trip on the three-mile steam railway through the woods.

Opposite Lakeside station and a mere 'stone's throw' from the Lake's edge you will find a the delightful **BOATERS BAR AND RES-TAURANT.** This newly refurbished, family run establishment prides itself in providing great tasting, home-cooked food, relaxing surround-ings and huge helpings of hospitality. The Windemere cruise ships dock nearby, so if your cruise has left you feeling peckish why not drop in for a delicious morning coffee, afternoon tea or a meal selected from the comprehensive menu which caters for all tastes and includes vegetarian dishes, an exciting choice of daily specials, children's meals and a tempting range of freshly prepared salads. There is ample car parking and good access for disabled persons.

Boaters Bar and Restaurant, Lakeside, Newby Bridge. Tel: 015395 31381

FINSTHWAITE is less than a mile from Lakeside, Here you will find **STOTT PARK BOBBIN MILL**, an early Victorian mill which has been beautifully restored as a working industrial monument and Visitor Centre, with a water-powered turbine and a steam-driven mill engine.

NEWBY BRIDGE, at the foot of Windermere, on the opposite shore from Lakeside, is where you will find **FELL FOOT COUNTRY PARK**, an area alongside the lake with lovely views, a playground and picnic areas.

Bowness is not all crowds and boats. Away from the marinas and the car parks is the old village, where **ST MARTIN'S CHURCH** is of particular interest. It has a magnificent East Window filled with 14th and 15th century glass and an unusual 300-year old wooden carved figure of St Martin, sharing his cloak with a beggar.

Windermere Steam Boat

Attractions that are well worth visiting in Bowness include the **WINDERMERE STEAM BOAT MUSEUM**, on the lake shore north of Bowness, with a unique collection of Victorian and Edwardian steam launches, including the 'S.L. Dolly', the oldest mechanically powered boat in the world.

Also **THE OLD LAUNDRY VISITOR CENTRE**, home of **THE WORLD OF BEATRIX POTTER**, an excellent walk-round centre with beautifully made tableaux of the Beatrix Potter characters and a handy coffee shop downstairs. The Old Laundry is also a centre for exhibitions, theatre and holiday activities (telephone 015394 88444).

Nestling in its own grounds at the foot of Lake Windermere, in the village of Newby Bridge, is **LYNDHURST COUNTRY HOUSE**, a charming early 20th century building. This family run hotel has gained an enviable reputation for friendliness and good service. All the five ensuite bedrooms offer the best in home comforts including TV, tea and coffee facilities and central heating. You may even find you have a luxury four poster bed. Accommodation is based on bed and breakfast, or dinner, bed and breakfast, and you can be sure of delicious home cooked food every mealtime. With ample, secure parking with room for boats and trailers, this is a super place to stay particularly if you are visiting the area with a mind to taking advantage of the various water and land sports available so close at hand.

Lyndhurst Country House, Newby Bridge Tel: 015395 31245

Nearby is the car ferry that links Bowness with **SAWREY**, on the opposite side of the lake, which is an attraction in itself, and an important form of transport - without it, travellers would have a long drive around the lake along winding lanes, to reach the villages of Hawkshead, Sawrey, Satterthwaite and Coniston. It's a very frequent service and approximate waiting times are posted on the approach roads.

UNDERBARROW village lies in a beautiful area of rolling hills about three or four miles between Bowness and Kendal. This area to the east of Lake Windermere is relatively little known, but it is delightful to explore, dotted with little hamlets, good country pubs and beautiful views across the rolling, hilly landscape.

Situated in beautiful area of rolling hills about three or four miles between Bowness and Kendal, lies the village of Underbarrow. In this area steeped in history and lying on the Old Woolpack Route, you will find **THE UNDERBARROW PUNCHBOWL**, a traditional English pub dating back to the 1500's. Run by former merchant navy officer, David Howarth, the Punchbowl is noted for traditional draft ales of which the Draft Bass was rated by the Daily Telegraph as the best pint in the North West. It is also renowned for its plentiful bar meals which are reasonably priced and available throughout the day. Adjoining the pub, David has established a caravan park where he lets caravans by the week. To the East of the Lake which is relatively little known, the pub itself is situated on the Westmorland Way walk and has some of the best walking on its doorstep. It is a delight to explore, with little hamlets and other interesting landmarks dotted along the route.

The Punchbowl, Underbarrow, Kendal, Cumbria. Tel: 01539 568234

CROOK Taking the more interesting B5284 route between Lake Windermere and Kendal, you arrive midway at the village of Crook. Nestling in a small soft valley with lovely panoramic views over the Crook countryside is **GLEBE HOUSE**, a former vicarage, but for the past fourteen years the home of Julia and Peter Young.

Glebe House

Built in Lakeland stone and with peaceful gardens enclosed by dry

145

stone walling, it is a welcoming place to spend a few days of your holiday. Two of the three letting rooms have en-suite facilities and the house generally has a warm and mellow feel to it. Julia will offer a large choice of breakfast options including vegetarian. You can pre-book sporting activities such as golf, riding and watersports, and you'll find the location ideally situated for touring Lakeland.

Glebe House, Crook, Kendal, Cumbria. Tel: 01539 821450

CROOK HALL, a historic 17th century farmhouse is set half a mile along a picturesque winding country lane, has lovely gardens and enjoys magnificent panoramic views of the surrounding countryside. Bonnie Prince Charlie is reputed to have stayed her whilst on his way to claim the English throne. Today this working farm offers B & B accommodation of a high standard and you can be sure of a 'right royal' welcome from Mr & Mrs Metcalfe, the owners. The lounge has original oak panelling and conceals a 'priesthole'. This fine farmhouse is ideally situated close to several country footpaths and a golf course, it is a good base from which to explore the area.

Crook Hall, Crook, Nr. Kendal, Cumbria. Tel: 01539 821352

Approximately six miles from both Kendal and Windermere, on the country road between Crook and Crosthwaite is **BULMAN STRANDS**; a working farm offering self-catering holidays in a choice of four well-equipped static caravans. Set in half an acre of grassland and orchard by the side of the River Gilpin, a favourite place for paddling and fishing for the children, there is plenty of space between the vans to allow for recreation.

The caravans are well positioned to take advantage of the good views and a variety of wildlife can be seen including Herons, Buzzards, deer and Squirrels. Nearby, there is a village shop, post office and telephone and within three miles of the farm is a choice of numerous Pubs serving meals. The accommodation is fully equipped and modern facilities for showers etc. are provided.

146

In 1374 this area was known as Bulleman Place in the parish of Crosthwaite from which it derives its name. A peaceful and tranquil setting yet close to all the main tourist routes. Approved by the English Tourist Board.

Bulman Strands, Crook, Kendal, Cumbria. Tel: 015395 68239

The Lyth Valley is famous for its damson orchards, white with blossom in Springtime and heavy with fruit in Autumn. Although a little off the popular 'beaten track', the unspoilt charm of this area makes is well worth a visit and **CROSTHWAITE HOUSE** is an ideal place to stay. Marnie and Robin Dawson, the resident proprietors, have many years experience in the hotel business in Lakeland.

Crosthwaite House

To reach Crosthwaite House take the A590 from the Kendal By-pass and turn right on to the A5074. After the Lyth Valley Hotel turn right and continue up the lane to the T-junction where you will find the house by turning left. From the attractive mid-18th century house there are superb views of the area. Inside, comfortable accommodation is offered in six en-suite bedrooms with tea and coffee-making facilities. The spacious residents' lounge has colour television and there is a 'no smoking' restaurant. If you prefer to be self-contained, book one of the self-catering cottages. Highly Commended by Tourist Board, you'll find here a welcoming atmosphere and good food.

Crosthwaite House, Crosthwaite, Nr. Kendal, Cumbria. Tel: 01539 568264

STAVELEY, now by-passed, is a village of great charm through which runs a stream crossed by footbridges. It lies at the foot of the little Kentmere Valley, a quiet cul-de-sac leading to the hamlet of KENTMERE itself. As its name implies, part of this valley was once a lake, drained to provide precious bottom pasture land. A large mill-pond remains to provide a head of water on the River Kent for use at a paper mill.

As many new By-pass roads are built for swifter progress, some established businesses unfortunately loose their prominence but benefit from the reduction of traffic noise. THE EAGLE AND CHILD is just such a place; a local village inn in Staveley at the foot of Kentmere Valley on the A591 between Kendal and Windermere. Its an excellent touring centre for walkers and motorists to the Lakes, Yorkshire Dales and Morecambe Bay areas; within a few yards you can join the Dalesway Walk. Lyn and Alan McCuaig are the well established owners of the Eagle and Child which was built in the 19th century and is mentioned in Dorothy Wordsworth's Journal. There are six letting bedrooms with Satellite television, hand basins, and tea making facilities. Bar meals are available at lunchtime and in the evening. Families are welcome and will find it well situated for bus and train services.

Eagle & Child, Staveley, Nr. Kendal, Cumbria. Tel: 01539 821320

On the main Windermere Road, in the heart of the village of Staveley, is the WEDGE HALL GALLERY AND TEA ROOM. The Gallery is a real Aladdin's cave with a wide range of pottery, hand turned wood, jewellery, dried flower arrangements, hand made toys and many other unusual and interesting gifts. As its name might suggest, Wedge Hall also has a fine display of original paintings and photographs as well as a selection of prints; many of the subjects include spectacular Lakeland scenery. In the same building, through the arches, is the tea room which offers a selection of teas and coffees and also a mouth-watering range of home made cakes and scones. If the weather is dry, refreshments are also served outside in the garden.

Wedge Hall Gallery and Tea Rooms, Windermere Road, Staveley
Tel: 01539 821130

This is a beautiful valley to explore on foot - a public path goes up the western side of the valley past **KENTMERE HALL**, a fortified pele tower, now a farmhouse. From the hamlet itself, where an ancient packhorse track climbs over **GARBURN PASS** to Troutbeck and Windermere, there is a spectacular walk, easily done by leaving a car at Windermere and using the train to return to Staveley.

THE RIVER KENT, which runs down into Kendal from Staveley via Burneside, carries the Dales Way from Yorkshire into the Lake District along its banks, an attractive stretch of riverside path, richly varied in character from mill-dam to rapids, and a haven for wildlife. Just south of Burneside, **THE RIVER SPRINT**, a tributary, meets the Kent. The Sprint has its own, remarkably beautiful **LONGSLEDDALE VALLEY** which curves past **GARNETT BRIDGE** deep into the high fell country. A bridle path climbs from the head of the valley into Kentmere, another spectacularly beautiful walk.

Equally little known, yet so very close to Windermere, is the countryside of THE WYNSTER VALLEY, south of Staveley, and THE LYTH VALLEY, which the main A5074 from Bowness, follows south to Levens. A network of narrow lanes links tiny hamlets like Wynster, Bowland Bridge and Underbarrow, across this area of low, spikey hills, not as spectacular as the central fells, but full of character and a special charm. There are some excellent pubs here too, off the beaten track, and well worth seeking out, especially the **MASON'S ARMS** at STRAW-BERRY BANK, which is listed in the Guinness Book of Records for selling the greatest number of different beers - over one hundred, including their own Damson beer, brewed on the premises. The Lyth Valley is also famous for its damson blossom in the Spring.

BOWLAND BRIDGE. Visitors to **LIGHTWOOD**, a delightful 17th century farmhouse near Bowland Bridge, in Cartmel Fell, will receive a warm welcome from hosts Evelyn and Fideo Cervetti.

Lightwood

This lovely home has been in Evelyn's family since 1945 and enjoys an idyllic location just 2 miles from the southern end of Lake Windermere. You can relax in the two acres of beautiful gardens, while inside you will find a cosy atmosphere with the oak beams and inglenook fireplaces retaining Lightwood's original charm. The accommodation comprises eight en-suite bedrooms, all beautifully furnished in keeping with the character of this lovely old farmhouse. As well as providing a wholesome breakfast, Evelyn and Fideo make your stay complete by offering a four-course dinner,(by arrangement), prepared using fresh homegrown produce. The house has its own spring water supply from a well in the gardens.

Lightwood Guesthouse, Cartmel Fell, Nr.Bowland Fell, Cumbria.
Tel: 01539 531454

The countryside west of Lake Windermere is an area of low, thickly wooded hills, most easily reached by taking the car ferry from Bowness to FAR SAWREY. Once across, the road takes you through NEAR SAWREY, a little village best known for another Lakeland celebrated literary figure, Beatrix Potter, whose home, **HILL TOP**, is now a National Trust property and a museum.

HAWKSHEAD lies at the head of Esthwaite Water. The village has changed little since William Wordsworth, at the age of eight, attended the Grammar School here, and it is all the better preserved since visitors are obliged to leave their cars outside the village centre and walk through it on foot. Next to the car park is the National Park Information Centre, a good starting point for exploring Hawkshead. A nice way to go into the village is past the Grammar School and through the churchyard. The 15th century church dominates Hawkshead from its high position, and is worth a look inside for its series of painted murals which date from 1680.

The footpath brings you out in the market square, enclosed by 17th

Grizedale Forest Sculpture

and 18th century shops and cottages.

The National Trust now owns some of the buildings in Hawkshead, including 'BEND OR BUMP', which was formerly a house and shop, and features in Beatrix Potter's "The Pie and the Patty Pan", and the former solicitor's office of William Heelis, who was Beatrix Potter's husband. This building is now **THE BEATRIX POTTER GALLERY**.

Hawkshead Town Trail takes you to these places, and to the cottage of Anne Tyson, where Wordsworth lodged as a student.

Some lovely walks lead from Hawkshead to **ROGER GROUND** and Esthwaite and to the nearby hamlet of COLTHOUSE, a group of fa msteads and cottages with a Quaker Meeting House built in 1688. One of the most interesting places to visit from Hawkshead is **GRIZEDALE FOREST**, famous for its Theatre and Sculpture. In the forest more than 100 sculptures have been commissioned over the last fifteen years, all made from natural materials found in the forest, and by some of Britain's best known contemporary artists, including the sculptor Andy Goldsworthy, as well as artists from all over the world. The great beauty of these sculptures is their understated presence - here you won't find any signposts pointing to the next exhibit, you are left entirely to your own devices to explore the wonders of this forest, with the help of a printed guide, either on foot or on mountain bike, which can be hired at the Visitor Centre.

The **THEATRE-IN-THE-FOREST** has an excellent programme throughout the year of musical and theatrical events of the highest quality, and the Visitor Centre now includes an art gallery and workshop which is also open to the public, where the artists in residence will happily take a break from their work to describe their experiences of living and working in this unique environment For details of "What's On" at the theatre, telephone 01229 860291

Grizedale Tea Rooms

In the heart of Grizedale Forest, at the Forest Park Centre, is the **GRIZEDALE TEA ROOMS**. Situated in the main centre complex, underneath the 'Theatre in the Forest', the tea rooms are ideally placed to quench the thirst of ramblers and thespians alike. With the other attractions of the Park Centre and the Grizedale Sculptures there is plenty to see and do. The tea rooms, run by Gaye Fletcher, are open all day, everyday, and offer a wide range of light lunches and cream teas as well as snacks and ice-creams. Surrounded by the sweet smelling air of the woods, and having worked up an appetite, it is a pleasure to enjoy the home-cooked, wholesome refreshments offered in this delightful setting.

SATTERTHWAITE nestles in the beautiful countryside of the Grizedale valley, between Coniston Water and Windermere Lake.

The small village of Satterthwaite is one of the remaining upspoilt areas of south Lakeland though it is only four miles from Hawkeshead. Situated in the village, with outstanding views down the Grizedale Valley, is **BOBTAIL COTTAGE**, a converted barn offering excellent self catering accommodation. Owned by Gaye Fletcher, the cottage is bright, spacious with large windows through which give panoramic views of the glorious surroundings. With Grizedale Forest so close the famous Theatre-in-the-Forest is only a mile away and the village pub is within walking distance.

Tastefully decorated throughout and featuring the original oak beams there is a large living room with dining area, a fully fitted kitchen with all the usual appliances including washer dryer, two bedrooms and a bathroom with shower. Outside the cottage has a small patio garden with furniture and a purpose built barbecue to make self catering more fun. With central heating, parking space and a phone this is a real home from home and an ideal base for a holiday, whatever the time of year. Not surprisingly Bobtail Cottage is an English Tourist Board Four Key Commended establishment.

Bobtail Cottage, Church Lane, Satterthwaite, Near Hawkeshead
Tel: 01229 860336

One of the most famous of all Lakeland valleys is of course, **LANGDALE**- steep, flat-bottomed and surrounded by towering peaks.

It is spectacularly beautiful, particularly the famous **LANGDALE PIKE** at the head of the valley above **DUNGEON GHYLL**, and is a mecca for hillwalkers and climbers.

Like so much of the Lake District this is an area best enjoyed on foot. There are easy paths along the valley floor all the way from **ELTERWATER** and **CHAPEL STILE** to **STICKLE TARN** or **BLEA TARN** at the head of the valley. Further walks, for the more experienced, lead to the summit of England's highest mountain, Scafell Pike, to Great Gable and other challenging peaks.

Strictly speaking, the valley most people refer to as Langdale is Great Langdale; the parallel valley is Little Langdale. A steep and narrow moorland road, Side Gate, links the two. At the head of Little Langdale is the **WRYNOSE PASS**, a murderously-steep road, not for the faint-hearted, over to the head of the Duddon Valley and the even steeper Hardknott Pass to **ESKDALE**.

THE DUDDON VALLEY, or Dunnerdale, which runs from **WRYNOSE BOTTOM** to **DUDDON SANDS**, is a particularly lovely, less well-known part of Lakeland. Richly wooded yet squeezed between high mountains, it has no major tourist attractions, just a landscape of rare quality. Immediately south of the little car park by **HINNING HOUSE** is the famous **BIRK'S BRIDGE**, an ancient pack-horse bridge in a perfect setting.

The road switchbacks down the valley to **SEATHWAITE**, which has a delightful church. Tucked away in this quiet little hamlet **THE NEWFIELD INN**, a charming, traditional inn run by two brothers, Andy and Chris Burgess. Here they serve three kinds of Theakston ales, including the very stong 'Old Peculiar', and also a selection of guest ales. The wholesome bar meals are excellent value and the portions are very generous, with favourites being the steaks, the large gammon, and the special steak pies.

The Newfield Inn

Adjacent to the inn Andy and Chris have two self catering flats which, like the inn, are open all year round and can sleep up to six people

Birk's Bridge, Dunnerdale

comfortably. This peaceful location in a totally unspoilt area of the Lake District is a walker's paradise, with ready access to Coniston Fell, the Furness Way and the Forestry Commission walks.

The Newfield Inn, Seathwaite, Broughton-in-Furness Tel: 01229 716208

ULPHA, the name meaning 'Wolf Hill'. There are some magnificent walks within and from this valley across the fells towards Ravenglass, Coniston or Torver.

CONISTON WATER is one of the more famous lakes yet one which is considerably less crowded than many of the others. Coniston Water is a gentler lake than Windermere, and the little town at its head, which shares its name, was once an important copper-mining centre. It is widely known for the beautiful decorative green slate, quarried locally, which is used on so many public buildings. You can still follow tracks from the centre of Coniston into the old copper-workings, long since closed. These provide part of the ascent of THE OLD MAN OF CONISTON, 2631ft above sea level and a fine viewpoint. Coniston is a pleasant, unpretentious little town with a small museum in memory of John Ruskin who lived at nearby Brantwood.

Coniston Water, because of its relative calmness, was used for water-speed record attempts. It has seen its share of triumph and tragedy in the careers of Malcolm Campbell and his son, Donald, who perished on the lake in an attempt to break the world record in 1967. A memorial to him is in the centre of Coniston village.

Happier association lies with memories of the author Arthur Ransome who used Coniston as a setting for his series of children's novels. PEEL ISLAND, at the south end of the lake, is the 'Wildcat Island' of the books.

But it is John Ruskin, the great art-historian, artist, moralist and critic who has perhaps the strongest links with Coniston. A narrow road, beautiful but not easy to drive along, will take you to BRANTWOOD around the far side of the Lake. The nicest way of getting there, however, is to take the superbly restored National Trust STEAM LAUNCH GONDOLA which cuts silently across the water as you enjoy the opulent luxury of its red velvet seats. Brantwood is more than just a shrine to Ruskin, the man who probably did more to create an awareness of the fine arts and architecture in Britain than any other. It is a magnificent country estate with a series of trails leading to superb view-points across Coniston Water to the surrounding hills. If you stand in Ruskin's study and share that incomparable view of the lake, you begin to understand just something of what motivated his genius. There is also a large car park and an excellent tearoom here within the old stables called 'Jumping Jenny', named after John Ruskin's boat.

Just a few miles south of Coniston, in the village of TORVER, there are some lovely walks, for instance across the fells into one of the Lake District's most tranquil 'hidden places', the Duddon Valley.

CHAPTER SEVEN

Furness

Holker Hall

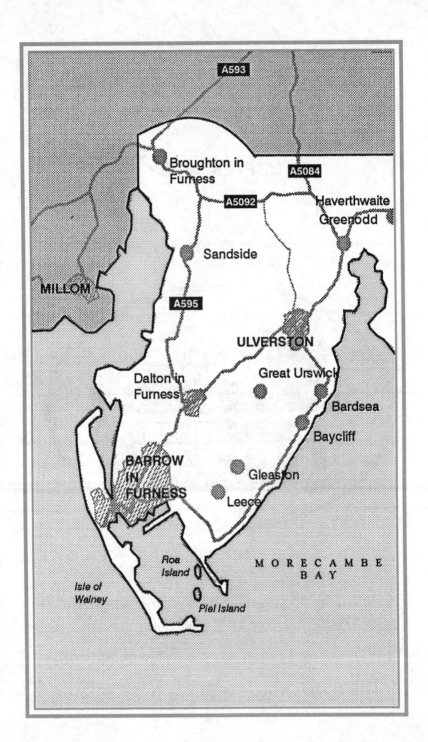

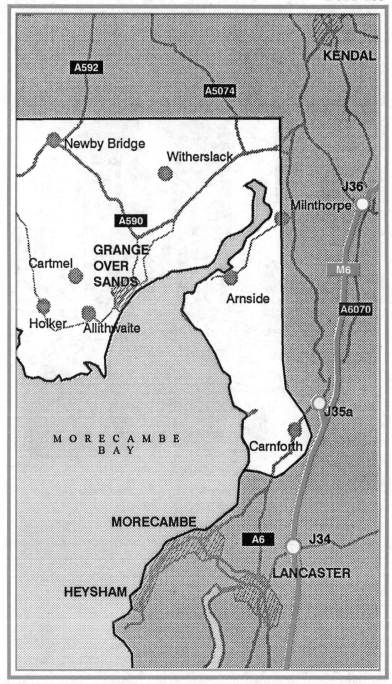

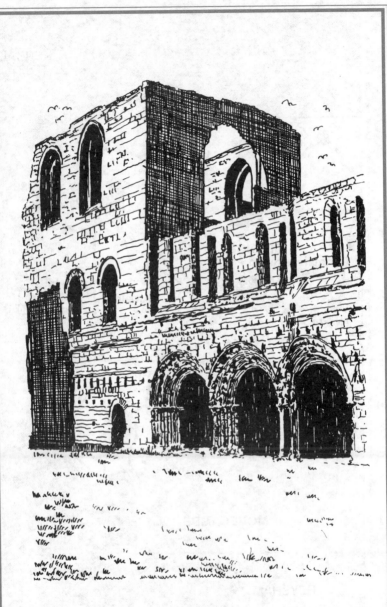

Furness Abbey

CHAPTER SEVEN

Furness

FURNESS lies between the lakes and mountains of Cumbria and the great sandy estuaries of Morecambe Bay. It is an area of gentle moorland, craggy headlands, scattered woodlands and vast expanses of sand. Once the stronghold of the Cistercian monks, their influence is still felt in the buildings and in the fabric of the landscape. It is well worth taking time to explore this part of Cumbria, both for the variety and distinctiveness of its countryside and its rich, exciting past.

DALTON, lying in a narrow valley on the part of Furness which extends deep into Morecambe Bay, is an ancient town which was once the leading town of Furness and an important centre for administration and justice.

The 14th-century pele tower, **DALTON CASTLE**, stands almost hidden by surrounding buildings. It was built around 1330-36 to provide a place of refuge for the monks of Furness Abbey against Scottish raiders. Over the centuries, in its twin role as both prison and court, it has been substantially altered internally, although it still retains most of its original external features. It is now owned by the National Trust and there is a small museum with an interesting display of 16th- and 17th-century armour.

Dalton became established as a market-town in the 13th century when the Cistercians began to hold fairs and markets in the town. Before the Dissolution of the Monasteries, it was the Abbot who held court and administered justice. Indeed, Dalton's decline coincided with the decline of the monks and the growing importance of Ulverston and Greenodd as ports.

The red sandstone **CHURCH OF ST. MARY** was designed by the celebrated Victorian architects Paley and Austin. In the graveyard lies George Romney (1734-1804), the famous portrait painter, who was born in the town.

Spend some time looking around the many fascinating facades in and around Market Place, such as the unique, cast-iron shop front at No 51, Market Street. In the Market Place itself is an elegant, Victorian drinking fountain, with fluted columns supporting a dome of open iron-work above the pedestal fountain. Nearby, stands the market cross and slabs of stone that were used for fish-drying in the 19th century.

As you pass through Dalton-in-Furness, the **GOLDEN BALL INN** is worth a visit particularly if you like Jazz, Folk or Rock music. The exterior has an attractive Tudor style upper frontage while the interior has been completely refurbished retaining its old style character. This is a lively establishment run by Steve, Sue and Robert where live music is featured three or four times a week. There's a very friendly atmosphere and a particularly warm welcome for any musicians calling in. Steve, himself a musician, plays regularly in the Golden Ball. Bar snacks are generally available to give sustenance and a beer garden at the rear offers a breath of air if you feel the need. Situated on Old Town Road through Dalton.

Golden Ball Inn, Ulverston Road, Dalton-in-Furness. Cumbria.
Tel: 01229 467757

To the south of Dalton is **FURNESS ABBEY**, a magnificent ruin of eroded red sandstone set in fine parkland, the focal point of South Cumbria's monastic heritage. You can still see the canopied seats in the presbytery and the graceful arches overlooking the cloister, testaments to the Abbey's former wealth and influence.

Furness Abbey stands in the **VALE OF DEADLY NIGHTSHADE**, a shallow valley of sandstone cliffs and rich pastureland. The Abbey itself was established in 1123 at Tulketh, near Preston, by Stephen, Count of Blois and King of England. Four years later it was moved to its present site and, after twenty years, became absorbed into the Cistercian Order. Despite its remoteness, the Abbey flourished with the monks establishing themselves as guides across the treacherous sands of Morecambe Bay. Rich endowments of land, which included holdings in Yorkshire and Ireland, led to the development of trade in products such as wool, iron and charcoal. It became the second wealthiest monastery in Britain after Fountains Abbey in Yorkshire.

After Dissolution in 1537 it became part of Thomas Cromwell's estate, and was allowed to decay into a picturesque and romantic ruin. It is now owned by English Heritage who have a small Interpretative Centre nearby detailing its history.

BARROW lies within walking distance of Furness Abbey, another Cumbrian contrast. Barrow is a 19th-century industrial town with long, narrow streets of terraced houses around a busy centre. Despite its industrial past, it has many features of interest.

Like other such towns in the last century, it grew up around a railway, built to transport locally-produced haematite (iron-ore), slate and limestone to a new deep-water port. Its original population was 200 but, by 1874, this had increased to over 35,000. However, it was steel production and ship-building that led to the town's real prosperity. James Ramsden established the first Barrow Iron Ship Company in 1870, taking advantage of local steel-production skills. In 1896 the firm was acquired by Vickers and for a number of years was the largest armaments works in the world.

You must still cross from Barrow Docks to WALNEY ISLAND by a bridge which joins the ten-mile long island to the peninsular. The island is reputedly the windiest lowland site in Britain and is well worth visiting. It contains two particularly important Nature Reserves.

NORTH WALNEY NATIONAL NATURE RESERVE has an area for the preservation of the Natterjack toad, Britain's rarest amphibian. Over 130 species of birds have been recorded here, with more than twenty nesting species. Its 350 acres exhibit a great variety of habitats including sand-dunes, heath, salt-marsh, sandy beaches, shingle and scrub. As well as having several species of orchid, it has the richest shingle-beach flora in the UK. North Walney's wildlife is matched by it rich prehistoric past with important archaeological sites from Mesolithic, Neolithic, Bronze and Iron Age times.

SOUTH WALNEY NATURE RESERVE, along the island's long foot, only reached by path, has the largest nesting ground of Herring Gulls and Lesser Black-backed Gulls in Europe. It is also the most southerly breeding point of such species as Oyster Catcher, Tern and Ringed Plover. It serves as a stop-over for many migratory birds and the Reserve is of considerable ecological interest with mudflats, sandy beaches, rough pasture, freshwater and brackish pools. For the visitor there are trails to follow and an observation building near the entrance. The southern tip of **WALNEY POINT** is dominated by a 70-ft lighthouse which was built in 1790 and originally provided light with an oil lamp. From **HAWS POINT**, there is a lovely view of Piel Island and its imposing Keep.

RAMPSIDE. Just as you enter the village of Rampside from the main road you will find **JESCROFT**. Taking four barns, the owners, Mr and Mrs Walker, have been sympathetically and cleverly converted them into self catering cottages that overlook the Irish Sea. This friendly couple have also tastefully decorated and furnished the cottages with antique and period furniture totally in keeping with the olde worlde feel generated by the oak beamed ceilings. All fully equipped with the latest in modern comforts children and family pets are welcome to join in the fun. This beautiful and secluded spot is the ideal place for a relaxing holiday or for touring the lakes.

Jescroft, Rampside Road, Rampside Tel: 01229 832177

THE WORDSWORTH HOUSE HOTEL is a residential hotel and restaurant enjoying magnificent panoramic views over Morecambe Bay. It has long be renowned for its superb food and hospitality, a tradition that Tony and Lynn Pearce, the owners are proud to maintain.

The Wordsworth House Hotel

The restaurant features a full a'la carte menu with a good selection and special vegetarian dishes and a children's menu. The hotel is beautifully decorated, with mahogany a feature in both the bar and the non-smoking restaurant. There are ten comfortable bedrooms all with en-suite facilities. Pets can be accommodated by prior arrangement. Directions - take the A5087 from Ulverston through Bardsea onto Rampside.

*The Wordsworth House, Rampside, Morecambe Bay, Cumbria. Tel: 01229
820303 Fax: 01229 820306*

ROA ISLAND is joined to the mainland by a causeway. If your journey takes you to Roa Island and the area of Barrow-in-Furness then why not take in a ferry trip to Piel Island and visit its castle. While waiting for the ferry, call in at **THE BOSUN'S LOCKER** where Lisa Hammond will welcome you to her neat cafe for morning coffee, hot meals and daytime snacks. The interior is furnished with wood and the tables have lace tablecloths. Enjoy special teas such as blackcurrant, passion fruit and apricot; there's home made cakes, cream teas and a special Sunday lunch. There's ice cream to take away and no doubt you'll want to call back later in the day. Nice friendly atmosphere.

*The Bosun's Locker, Roa Island, Nr. Barrow-in-Furness, Cumbria.
Tel: 0585 641758*

PIEL ISLAND is reached by ferry from Roa Island which is joined to the peninsular by a causeway. Piel Island was probably visited by the Celts and later by the Romans, but its first recorded name is Scandinavian 'Fotheray', from Old Norse meaning 'fodder island'. In 1127 the island was given to the Savignac Monks by King Stephen as part of their original land-grant for an Abbey. After the Savignacs merged with the Cistercians in the middle of the 12th century, Furness Abbey began to use the island as a warehouse and storage area, being both near to the Abbey and a safe harbour.

The motte-and-bailey CASTLE on the island, built in the early part of the 14th century, was the largest of its kind in the north-west. It was intended to be used as a fortified warehouse protected against attacks from pirates and sea-raiders. However, in later years it also proved to be a useful defence against the King's Customs men and a prosperous trade in smuggling began.

One of the most exciting events in Piel's history occurred on June 4th, 1487 when Lambert Simnel, a merchant's son, landed on the island. Simnel had claimed he was the Earl of Warwick (one of the Princes in the Tower said to have been murdered by Richard III) and therefore the rightful King of England. With an army of German and Irish mercenaries, Simnel set out across Furness to march to London. However, when he arrived in London it was as the prisoner of Henry VII, having been defeated by the King's forces at the Battle of Stoke.

Lambert Simnel's name lives on in Piel, where the landlord of THE SHIP INN is traditionally known as 'King', after Simnel's claim to the title. In the Ship Inn is an old oaken chair and anyone who sits on it becomes a 'Knight of Piel'. The knighthood ceremony must be performed either by the 'King' or another 'Knight'. Following this the new 'Knight' is required to buy everyone a drink! A 'Knight' must be a moderate smoker, an ardent lover of the opposite sex and of good character. One of the rights of the 'Knight', if he is ship-wrecked on Piel, is that he may go to the inn and demand free lodgings and as much as he can eat and drink! When the tide is out there is the opportunity to walk to the Ship Inn on Piel Island for a drink - or several if you are marooned!

This part of Furness has many small hamlets and villages, such as LEECE, BAYCLIFF, SLAITH and GLEASTON. Each has its own identity and all can be reached from the beautiful Furness coast road, the A5087.

GLEASTON WATER MILL is a renovated corn mill, which has been lovingly restored by its present owners. The mill contains working machinery and is now a centre of local crafts and country cooking, an extremely handy place for a well-earned rest. It is well worth paying a visit to the man in THE LEATHER SHOP who makes superb hand-painted leather belts.

ALDINGHAM, along the coast road, is reputed to have once been washed away by a tidal wave, but no one is quite sure of the truth of this story. However, do visit the CHURCH OF ST. CUTHBERT, said to be

Piel Castle

one of the many places where the monks of Jarrow rested the Saint's body in their flight from the Danes. Inside the Church there is a charming statue of St Cuthbert with his otters, which was presented by Durham Cathedral. Parts of the Church date from the 12th century and there are some interesting old pieces of sculpture in the north aisle. Notice the crooked chancel arch, a feature occasionally found in old churches, meant to represent the body of Christ with his head leaning to one side. There is a hagioscope (window) in the wall to allow parishioners sitting in the south aisle to view the altar.

GREAT URSWICK. The ancient **CHURCH OF ST. MARY AND ST. MICHAEL** has a hagioscope. However, the great joy of this church is its unusual and lively woodcarvings by the Chipping Camden Guild of Carvers. Of particular note is the figure of a pilgrim, to the left of the chancel arch, and the small carvings in the choir-stall of winged children playing musical instruments. Look out for the three-decker pulpit with its scallop-shaped sounding board and the 9th-century wooden cross with a runic inscription. A rush-bearing ceremony is held in the church every September.

The road from Great Urswick leads on to **BIRKRIGG COMMON**, a lovely area of open land with a Bronze Age circle and superb views of the Bay. At Sunbrick, on the edge of the Common, in the churchyard, is the unmarked grave of Margaret Fell who married George Fox, one of the founders of the Quaker movement.

LITTLE URSWICK. Just five miles south of the quaint cobbled market town of Ulverston near the charming and quiet village of Great Urswick you will find **BOLTON MANOR FARM**.

Bolton Manor Farm

This large working dairy farm, owned by M and D Stable, also has an attractive and spacious first floor holiday apartment, in the large farmhouse, which makes a wonderful base for a self catering, family holiday. The apartment has a fully fitted kitchen, modern bathroom, large bedroom and a spacious lounge with bed settee and magnificent views over the surrounding countryside. Ideally situated close to the

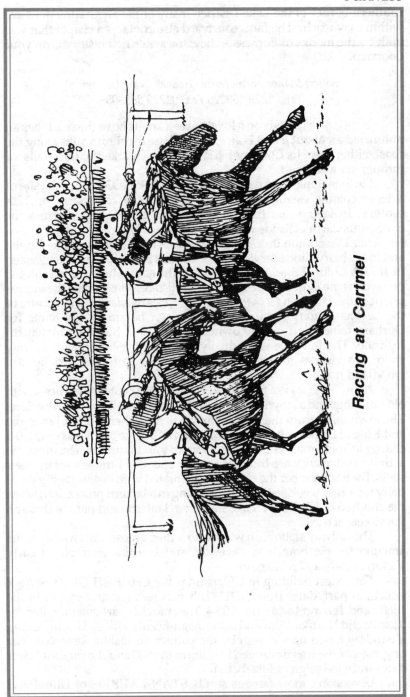

Racing at Cartmel

southern border of the Lake District, many of the areas attractions are within easy reach. The farm courtyard also contains a chapel that was built by the monks of Furness Abbey; the area's rich history is on your doorstep.

Bolton Manor Farm, Little Urswick, Near Ulverston
Tel: 01229 869228 Fax: 01229 869905

BARDSEA, stands on a lovely green knoll above the sea. It has an unhurried air about it and is an excellent base for short walks along the coast, either from its Country Park, along waymarked nature trails, or through its woodland.

Further along the coast is **CONISHEAD PRIORY**, once the site of a leper colony, established by the Augustinian canons in the 12th century. In later years the monks used to act as guides across the dangerous Cartmel Sands which formed the only direct road to Lancaster. After Dissolution in 1539, a fine private house was built on the site and the Estuary Guide service was continued by the Duchy of Lancaster. In 1821, a Colonel Braddyll demolished the earlier house and built the present ornate Gothic mansion. He was also responsible for the atmospheric ruined folly on CHAPEL ISLAND, clearly visible in the centre of the Levens Estuary. Conishead Priory later became a rest-home for Durham miners but is now owned by the Tibet Buddhist Manjushri Institute. The Institute is gradually restoring the house and warmly welcomes visitors for tours of the house, or to follow a delightful woodland trail.

ULVERSTON is a fine market town in the centre of Furness, with old buildings and a labyrinth of cobbled streets and alleyways to explore. The town dates from the 12th century when Stephen, Earl of Boulogne and King of England, owned the Manor. In 1280 the town was granted a charter to hold a market and every Thursday and Saturday it bustles with activity as livestock are brought for sale and street-traders set up their stalls. Each September the charter is celebrated with events taking place daily for a two-week festival, culminating in a lantern procession, when the children of Ulverston make their own lanterns and parade through the streets at dusk.

The railway station, on what is now the Furness Line, was once the junction for the branch to Lakeside, and is a fine example of early Victorian railway architecture.

The oldest building in Ulverston is the **CHURCH OF ST MARY** which, in part, dates from AD1111. It was restored and rebuilt in the 1860's and a chancel added in 1903-4. The church is particularly noted for its splendid Norman door and some magnificent stained glass, including a window based on a design by the painter Sir Joshua Reynolds. The original steeple was destroyed in a storm in 1540 and the present tower dates from the reign of Elizabeth I.

Ulverston's most famous son is **STAN LAUREL**, of Laurel and

Hardy fame, who was born here in 1890. His real name was Arthur Stanley Jefferson and he spent his first fifteen years in a small terraced house, **No. 3 ARGYLL STREET**. It now has a plaque commemorating him and a local pub has been renamed 'The Stan Laurel'. Nearby, at Upper Brook Street, is the **LAUREL AND HARDY MUSEUM**, crammed with photographs and relics of the comedian and his Hollywood partner, Oliver Hardy.

    LONSDALE HOUSE is an elegant 18th century hotel with its own mature secluded garden bordered by the historic 'Daltongate Folly'. Although it is situated opposite the Market Cross in the bustling town centre of Ulverston, the hotel and gardens have a genteel, peaceful and friendly atmosphere in which you will find it easy to unwind and enjoy a relaxing stay. It is probably for this reason that the hotel has become popular with VIPs and celebrities. The cuisine, as you would expect, is excellent. Full English or continental breakfast is available each morning, bar meals are served at lunchtime and in the evening dinner is served in the tasteful dining room, where you can choose from the extensive a ia carte or menu of the day. A good selection of quality wines is always available. The comfortable lounge bar and residents lounge are the ideal places to relax with an after dinner drink. The spacious bedrooms are individually furnished and all have en-suite bathrooms. Each bedroom is centrally heated and equipped with a direct-dial phone, colour television, trouser press, hair dryer and tea and coffee making facilities. Tourist Board 4 Crown commended.

Lonsdale House Hotel, 11 Daltongate, Ulverston. Tel:01229 582598

    SWARTHMOOR, on the outskirts of Ulverston, is a small collection of white-washed cottages and a 16th century hall. **SWARTHMOOR HALL** stands in a well-kept garden and, although a cement rendering disguises its antiquity, the mullioned windows and leaded panes give a clue to its age. It was built around 1586 by George Fell, a wealthy landowner and it was his son, Judge Thomas Fell, who was to marry Margaret Askew. In 1652 Margaret Fell heard George Fox preach and became convinced of 'The Truth'. However, many were suspicious of Fox's beliefs and he was to suffer rough treatment and persecution. Margaret was able to persuade her husband to use his position to give Fox protection and shelter, and the Hall became the first settled centre of the Quaker sect, the place where missionaries were organised. A library was started with both Quaker and anti-Quaker literature. Judge Fell died in 1658 and eleven years later Margaret married George Fox. The Hall is now open in the summer months and gives a fascinating insight into the history of the early Quakers.

BROUGHTON-IN-FURNESS is another delightful part of West Cumbria which deserves to be better known. This charming little market town, built on the side of a hill above the Duddon Valley, is filled with handsome 18th-century houses.

THE MARKET HALL still has its original 1766 clock. The Market Square, from where the Market Charter is still proclaimed annually, has its original stone-slabbed stalls.

JACK HADWIN'S MOTOR CYCLE COLLECTION, in the OLD TOWN HALL, boasts fifty machines dating from between 1899 to 1959 as well as items from the early days of motoring.

Broughton is an ideal base from which to explore the Duddon Valley and the relatively little-known fell-country all around, as well as the coast and northern Furness. And there are many surprises. About two miles west of Duddon Bridge, high up on Swinside Fell, and only reached by footpath, is SWINSIDE STONE CIRCLE, sometimes known as 'Sunkenkirk'. This prehistoric monument could be 3500 years old, and was built for a purpose that can only be guessed at.

GREENODD, east of Broughton and north of Ulverston, is now a quiet village overlooking the Levens Estuary but it was once a major port with space for up to fifty ships. Stone, metal and ores produced in the Furness fells were transported from here to all over the world.

Summer Hill Holidays

If you enjoy getting away from it all in a quiet and secluded spot, you need look now further than SUMMER HILL HOLIDAYS. In the Crake Valley, at SPARK BRIDGE near Ulverston, Brian and Rosemary

Campbell have the most wonderful and imaginative self catering holiday accommodation you could wish to find. In the mature grounds of their Grade II listed Georgian house there are four two bedroomed timber lodges. Beautifully furnished and decorated, with the latest kitchen equipment and bathroom fittings, each lodge has a verandah overlooking the gardens. As part of the main house there is a cottage and a flat, suitable for disabled guests, which both offer a similar high standard of comfort. Rosemary and Brian take great care in ensuring that each and every guest enjoys their stay to the full. Putting themselves in their guests' position they have a range of extra services, such as frozen home cooked meals and groceries ready for your arrival, that make all the difference between a good holiday and a great one.

Summer Hill Holidays, Spark Bridge, Near Ulverston Tel: 01229 861510

HAVERTHWAITE, to the east, is the start of the **HAVERTHWAITE AND LAKESIDE RAILWAY,** which operates a steam train along the River Leven to Lake Windermere.

In the **CHURCH OF ST ANNES** a mural tablet tells the tragic story of George Dickinson killed in Montevideo by a shot fired at another man. The bullet passed through the target's body but accidentally killed Dickinson.

Leaving Haverthwaite in the direction of Kendal, turn right onto the B5278, a country road which follows the sandy coast through the villages of HOLKER and CARK, where the magnificent railway viaduct on the coast line crosses the Levens Estuary to the fishing village of FLOOKBURGH

Lakeland Trekking

LAKELAND TREKKING near the village of Flookburgh just south of the Lake District offers a wide variety of horse rides with something suit beginners and the more experienced rider whatever their age. With over thirty horses, and with all training under the supervision of professional instructors, there is a horse for everyone. The riding school itself has a large outdoor arena for jumping and dressage lessons and, with some wonderful countryside just minutes away, there are a range of trail rides available. Fast beach rides across the sand to Chapel Island or long distance trail rides through the Grizedale Forest and the Lakeland Fells, this is certainly an exhilarating way to discover the area.

Lakeland Trekking, Moor Lane, Flookburgh, Near Grange-over-Sands
Tel: 015395 58131

Forty eight years ago, Dick Taylor opened a little Nursery growing lettuces and tomatoes. Today, **SOUTHERN LAKELAND NURSERIES** has grown to a large and successful garden centre specialising in pot plants, bedding plants and hardy plants, under half an acre of glass housing. There are outdoor gardens as well as undercover areas, a shop supplying all types of garden sundries and a cafe. Dick and his wife Joan, ably assisted by their son Michael, look after the day to day running of the garden centre while daughter Alison and her helpers run the cafe and do all the cooking. It is open for delicious home cooked food, teas, coffees, salads, cakes and snacks seven days a week. As you walk around the Centre, you will find a huge variety to choose from and a member of the family will usually be on hand to assist with help and information. While you're there, why not send some flowers to a friend or relative through their Interflora service. Located opposite Railway Station on B5278 a quarter mile from Holker Hall.

Southern Lakeland Nurseries, Cark-in-Cartmel, Grange-over-Sands,
Cumbria. Tel: 015395 58237

Nearby is **HOLKER HALL**, formerly home of the Dukes of Devonshire and now lived in by the Cavendish Family, set in a splendid country estate and deer-park. It is famous for one of the best private libraries in England with over 3,500 volumes. It also has exquisite interiors with fine wood-carvings ad decorated ceilings. Here you will find an embroidered panel, said to have been worked by Mary, Queen of Scots, a Victorian and Edwardian Kitchen exhibition and an animal house. There is also the **LAKELAND MOTOR MUSEUM** with a superb collection of over 100 veteran or vintage vehicles. The grounds are also a delight and a whole

The Gatehouse, Cartmel Priory

day can easily be spent here.

CARTMEL, is a short walk from Holker Hall, by footpath. This is one of the prettiest villages in Furness. Cartmel is a delightful cluster of houses and cottages set around a square, from which lead winding streets and arches into charming back yards. The village is dominated by the famous **CARTMEL PRIORY**, founded in 1188 by Augustine Canons. According to legend, it was originally intended to be sited on nearby Mount Barnard, but St Cuthbert appeared in a vision to the monastic architect and ordered him to build the Priory between two springs of water. Next morning the foundation stones were to be found trickling in opposite directions and this is where the Church stands today.

Like all such monastic institutions, the Priory was disbanded in 1537 and several of its members were executed for participating in the Pilgrimage of Grace. Today, only the 14th century gatehouse and the **CHURCH OF ST MARY AND ST MICHAEL** have survived. Indeed, after the dissolution, only the south aisle was used as a parish church, but in 1620 George Preston of Holker began to restore the entire building, re-roofing it and presenting the church with the richly-carved black oak screens and stall canopies.

Apart from its glorious east window, one of its most noticeable features is the unique tower set diagonally on the tower stage. Inside, in the south-west corner of the church, is a door known as **CROMWELL'S DOOR**. The holes in it are said to have been made by indignant parishioners firing at Cromwellian soldiers who had stabled their horses in the nave. Parliamentary troops were in the area in 1643 and, indeed, fragments of lead were found in the wood during restoration work in 1955.

Situated in the main square is **THE ROYAL OAK**, the oldest pub in Cartmel. It has changed very little in 400 years, apart from its name which changed from 'The Punch Bowl' to 'The Royal Oak' in 1736. The pub is reputed to have been built from the remains of some farm buildings which were destroyed in 1537.

Today this fine pub is popular with locals and visitors alike. The

Cartmel

atmosphere is very friendly, and you can be sure of a warm welcome from Steve, the landlord. A good selection of real ales is kept on draught, reasonably priced bar meals are also available. Families are made most welcome.

The Royal Oak, The Square, Cartmel, Grange-over-Sands, Cumbria.
Tel: 015395 36259

Situated in Cartmel's village square is **COUNTRY CLASSICS**, a 'hidden place' well worth seeking out. This fine clothing shop is housed in a Virginia Creeper clad Grade II listed building and is run by Ian and Karen Conroy, who pride themselves on the quality of the clothes that they stock and the high standard of friendly and informal service which they offer.

Country Classics

The shop stocks classic style clothing ranges for all; ladies clothes by Jinique, mens clothes by Pegasus and children's clothes by Applique and Scallywag. A good range of men's, ladies' and children's shoes are also stocked. Why not call in for a rummage, you are sure to find something to suit you (and your purse). Open all day every day.

Country Classics, The Square, Cartmel, Grange Over Sands.
Tel: 015395 36165

Tucked away off the village square, in a small courtyard behind the medieval priory is **COURTYARD COTTAGE**. This delightful stone built cottage was once a stable block, but has recently been sensitively converted to provide a high standard of accommodation. It is available for self catering breaks all year round and is ideally placed as a base for exploring all of the places described in this book.

The accommodation consists of; a well equipped kitchen (including a gas hob & electric oven), dining hall and two single bedrooms (cots are available) with a bathroom on the ground floor and, on the first floor; a double bedroom with private washing facilities and a generously sized lounge which enjoys a superb view of the priory. A TV and Video and a selection of games are also provided for guests to use.

The garden has a small patio area and there is a private parking space. Well behaved pets are welcome. ETB 4 keys commended

Courtyard Cottage, The Square, Cartmel. Tel: 015395 36165

Cartmel also has a charming **RACE COURSE** and any Tourist Information Centre will give details of the meetings held here.

Just outside Cartmel lies the small, quiet, family owned and run **GREAVES FARM CARAVAN PARK**. All the twenty static vans are pleasantly situated amongst orchard trees on level grass sites. Fully serviced with water and electricity, with shower, refrigerator and running hot water these vans are very suitable for family holidays. The Park also welcomes touring vans and tents though as space is limited it is advisable to book in advance. As well as offering the vans for self-catering holiday hire, the Rigg family also have available a charming bungalow set in its own garden just a short walk away from the Park. So close to the southern Lakes and the Morecambe Bay area, this is a wonderful spot for a family break.

Greaves Farm Caravan Park, Field Broughton, Grange-over-Sands
Tel: 015395 36329

A mile from the historic village of Cartmel and overlooking Morecambe Bay, is the impressive **UPLANDS HOTEL.** Uplands was opened in 1985 by Tom and Diana Peter, with John Tovey of the renowned Miller Howe Hotel in Windermere. Tom and Diana both worked with John at Miller Howe before opening Uplands. As you might imagine, the food is terrific but also worth noting is the warm, friendly and informal atmosphere of the place. As well as the restaurant, the hotel has five ensuite bedrooms, all comfortably furnished and prettily decorated. Standing in over two acres of delightful gardens, with magnificent views of the Leven Estuary, this is particularly special place to enjoy a meal and spoil yourself.

Uplands Country House Hotel, Haggs Lane, Cartmel
Tel: 015395 36248 Fax 015395 36848

ALLITHWAITE was founded by the Vikings, and originally called 'Lilifr's Thwaite', thwaite being the Westmorland word for 'a clearing'. In the 17th century it boasted a corn mill, and later a brewery, now converted into pretty cottages.

Within the old manor of Allithwaite is Humphrey Head where, in the 18th and 19th centuries, visitors flocked to sample the waters of the Holy Well. The Yorkshire and Cumberland miners thought the waters would heal the illnesses caused by their work.

GRANGE-OVER-SANDS was once a small coastal village, which was transformed into a fashionable resort by the coming of the Furness Railway linking it with Lancaster. Villas and hotels were built to take advantage of the exceptionally mild climate. Though the sands are not safe for bathing, this is more than compensated by the extensive promenade gardens along the sea-front. Due to the mild climate these boast rock-plants, alpines and even subtropical species. Away from the hotels, shops and cafes there are some lovely walks, none nicer than the path behind the town which climbs through the magnificent limestone woodlands, rich in wild flowers.

The path leads to **HAMPSFELL SUMMIT** and **THE HOSPICE,** a little stone tower from which there is an unforgettable view of Morecambe Bay and the craggy peaks of the Lake District. The Hospice was provided by a pastor of Cartmel in the last century for the 'shelter and entertainment of wanderers'. An external flight of stairs leads to a flat roof and the viewing-point. See if you can work out the riddle scrawled on one of the walls! Grange is also the starting point of the **'CISTERCIAN WAY'**, an exceptionally interesting, thirty-seven mile footpath route through Furness to Barrow, linking many sites of Cistercian interest.

The road through Grange joins up with the A590, where it is worth taking a left turn to **HIGH NEWTON** for more dramatic views across the Kent Estuary which is spanned by a fifty-arch railway viaduct. It was built by the engineer James Brunless in 1856-7, who used deep-sunk iron piles on broad circular discs to hold the structure firm amidst the treacherous Kent quicksands. The Estuary is a haven for wildlife with over 133 species of birds having been recorded in recent years.

Just off the main A590 route between the M6 motorway and Grange, and only 20 minutes drive from the heart of the Lake District, you will find the **DERBY ARMS**, Witherslack. This country inn, which dates back to the early 19th century, has a cosy, warm atmosphere. Open all day, everyday, your host, Stewart Farrer, serves a superb range of fine, traditional ales and tasty, home cooked bar meals are available at lunchtime and in the evening and the traditional Sunday lunch is always popular. The Derby Arms is also a residential inn offering guests a high standard of comfort in each of the five bedrooms. With an purpose built children's play area and some fine countryside right on its doorstep this is a super place to stop.

Derby Arms, Witherslack Tel: 015395 52207

LINDALE. Here you will find **THE LINDALE INN**, a charming, old coaching inn at the crossroads in the centre of this small village, near Grange. Renowned for serving the *'Best Steaks in the Lakes'*, the inn also has a full menu of traditional pub food, mouthwatering grills, salads and, of course, Cumberland sausage. Your hosts, Nick and Jane Kirkpatrick, also have an extensive range of malt whiskies behind the bar and serve a selection of fine ales.

With five, ensuite bedrooms, all decorated to a high standard, this is an ideal place to stay. As well as visiting Lindale Inn, do take a look at **THE JOHN WILKINSON MEMORIAL**, near the crossroads. The tall obelisk, made from black iron, commemorates the life of this local man, who invented the iron boat, and has been all but forgotten by historians and engineers alike.

The Lindale Inn, Lindale, Grange-over-Sands Tel: 015395 32416

ARNSIDE, on the far bank of the Kent Estuary is a quiet town with a short but elegant promenade. Once a busy port with its own ship-building and sea-salt refining industries, the silting up of the estuary in the 19th century saw its decline. With Grange and nearby Silverdale (in Lancashire), it is now a favourite retirement destination and a quiet holiday resort.

Around Arnside itself there is a wonderful choice of country walks, particularly over and around **ARNSIDE KNOTT**. This limestone headland, now a Nature Reserve rich in old woods and wild flowers, is part of the Arnside and Silverdale Area of Outstanding Natural Beauty. Knott comes from the Saxon word meaning 'rounded hill', which in this case rises 521ft above sea level and gives extensive views of the Lakeland fells, the Pennines and the coast. There is a beautiful path around the headland and along the shoreline past **BLACKSTONE POINT**. If you continue inland by quiet lanes or footpaths you soon reach **ARNSIDE TOWER**, another 14th-century pele tower. This particular one was built around 1375, during the reign of Edward III. It may have been part of the chain of towers designed to form a ring of protection for Morecambe Bay.

SILVERDALE. If you are a keen gardener, just a beginner, or simply enjoy admiring beautiful gardens then you will find that the **WATERSLACK FARM GARDEN CENTRE** is well worth a visit. Hidden away in beautiful countryside and surrounded by National Trust woodland, this garden centre is acclaimed by many to be the prettiest on the Cumbria-Lancashire border and it's not difficult to see why, for its plant displays are always superbly presented. The centre not only stocks a wide and varied range of plants and shrubs, but also possesses a lovely tea room where you can enjoy a delicious, home cooked light lunch or an afternoon tea. You may be tempted to try one of the many mouth-watering Austrian gateaux or home baked cakes which are also on offer. In the same building is a delightful gift shop which stocks all manner of country gifts. The Waterslack Garden Centre is situated near to the Leighton Moss Bird Reserve and Leighton Hall, on the road to Arnside. The garden centre is open every day from 8.00am. to 5.30pm., the tea room is open every day from 10.00am. to 5.30pm. and is closed on Mondays and Tuesdays during the winter.

Waterslack Garden Centre, Tea Room and Gift Gallery, Silverdale.
Garden Centre Tel: 01524 701255   Tea Room Tel: 01524 701862

WARTON. THE SHOVEL INN in Warton is the epitome of the traditional English public house. Interestingly however, the building was not constructed as a pub, but was originally a Court House dating from the 16th century.

The Shovel Inn, Warton

In 1792 it became a public house and was firstly called 'The Malt Shovel'. Apparently became popular with travellers on the main coach route into Kendal. Today the pub retains its popularity and its 16th century character and now boasts a beer garden and an aviary. A good selection of ales are kept and bar snacks are also available. The Shovel Inn is easily found on Main Street in the centre of Warton.

The Shovel Inn, 66 Main Street, Warton. Tel: 01524 733745

BEETHAM, on the A6 further North, has an unusual 19th-century **POST OFFICE** with a distinctive black-and-white studded door. Within earshot of a waterfall is the **CHURCH OF ST MICHAEL AND ALL ANGELS**, approached through a pergola of rambling roses. The church dates from Saxon times and, during restoration work in 1834, a hoard of about a hundred old coins was discovered at the base of a pillar. The coins were from the reigns of Edward the Confessor, William the Conqueror and William Rufus. In the Civil War, the church was badly damaged, its windows smashed and effigies broken. However, a glass fragment of Henry IV in an ermine robe has survived.

Tucked away in the heart of the delightful village of Beetham is the charming **WHEATSHEAF HOTEL**. Overlooking Beetham's historic Norman church, the Hotel has been run by Margaret Shaw and her parents before her, for the past 30 years, and was originally built in 1609 as a coaching inn. It was ideally situated, lying only 100 yards off the A6, which was then the main road linking the South to Scotland, and it allowed travellers to rest and refresh themselves whilst the horses were changed.

The Wheatsheaf Hotel

The Wheatsheaf is a popular and busy hotel, full of character, and although it has been obviously updated and refurbished, it has retained its original charm and exudes a warm, friendly atmosphere. The bar offers a wide choice of fine ales, and a varied selection of bar meals are available daily. On the first floor there is a cosy, intimate restaurant which provides an excellent, reasonably priced menu, including a variety of home-made pies and hotpots, tasty roasts, fresh fish and freshly made fruit tarts and meringue dishes, as well as an extensive cold buffet. Its popularity makes prior bookings advisable for weekend evenings or Sunday lunchtime. In addition to the fine fare on offer, Margaret also provides top class accommodation. There are six letting bedrooms, all en-suite, spacious and with that little extra personal touch, which make The Wheatsheaf a lovely place to stay. Downstairs visitors should look out for the showcase which houses a vast selection of dolls that have been collected from all over the world.

The Wheatsheaf Hotel, Beetham, Near Milnthorpe Tel: 01539 562123

HERON CORN MILL, close by, is a restored and working water-mill, with fully operational grinding machinery. It is a good example of a traditional corn mill which operated for trade in a Westmorland farming area, and only ceased trading in 1955. The situation of Heron Mill is ideal, because a natural shelf of rock in the river Bela forms a waterfall, providing the necessary head of water to drive the waterwheel. This made the site an obvious one when, in 1220, the Lords of the Manor of Haverback granted lands to the Canons of Coningshead for the erection of a corn mill. It is referred to several times in archives from the middle ages, and the land was transferred to Sir William Thorneburghe when Coningshead was destroyed at the Dissolution of the Monasteries in 1538. There is an exhibition about its history and the processes of milling.

SANDSIDE sits on the banks of the Kent estuary, where in the Middle Ages, heavily-laden pack horses and drovers with sheep and cattle used to make hazardous crossings making their way up the coast into Cumbria, rather than taking the longer, but safer route via Levens.

Heading north from Beetham along the A6, a turning to the left at Milnthorpe takes you onto the B5282, and after a mile or so, brings you to the **SHIP INN**, which stands on a sharp bend in the road at Sandside.

The Ship Inn

The building dates from the 17th century and takes its name from the ships which once transported iron ore across the bay from here. formerly a coaching inn, it has been a pub for over 130 years and at one time brewed its own beer. Inside, a warm welcome awaits you from Margaret and Dave Forrester, who are justly proud of the friendly atmosphere, oak-beamed ceilings and interesting 19th century graffiti on the windows. Top quality food is served in the spacious lounge bar every lunchtime and evening, and there is also a pleasant games room and a large children's adventure playground to the rear.

The Ship Inn, Sandside, near Milnthorpe. Tel: 015395 63113

MILNTHORPE has been a market town since the 14th century. The River Bela runs by its side, past the comb mill - which makes combs from synthetic material these days, rather than horn or ivory as it used to - and through **DALLAM TOWER PARK** to meet up with the mouth of the River Kent.

CHAPTER EIGHT

The South Cumbrian Coast

Calder Abbey

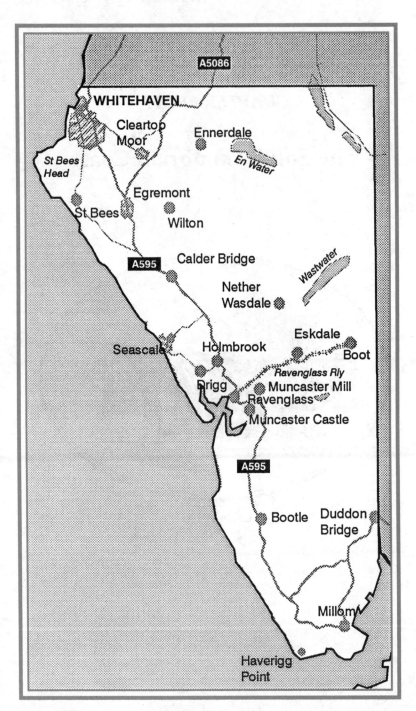

CHAPTER EIGHT

The South Cumbrian Coast

The section of Cumbria's coast and hinterland stretching down from St Bees Head to the Duddon Estuary has its own identity and quiet charm. It is a coast dominated by small, 19th century, iron-mining communities set against the romantic outline of the Lakeland Fells and the grey-blue waters of the Irish Sea. This area is most brilliantly captured in the verse and prose of Millom poet, Norman Nicholson.

MILLOM stands at the mouth of the River Duddon on the banks of the estuary, with the 1970ft **BLACK COMBE FELL** behind it. Like neighbouring towns in this region, it grew with the development of the iron industry, and the town's **FOLK MUSEUM** tells its history. The Museum also contains a permanent memorial to Norman Nicholson which tells of his books of verse and prose on local life and customs.

The 200 year old **KING WILLIAM IV** pub close to Kirksanton's stone circle is a 'hidden place' not to be missed. Just 10 minutes walk to a quiet fine sand and shingle beach, 2 miles from a nature reserve, bird sanctuary and the local railway station, this well located pub offers a wide selection of real ales and an extensive menu consisting of 28 main course dishes. There are plenty of popular desserts with which to follow your main course, these include very popular sticky toffee pudding and delicious home-made ginger cake. Roger and Sandra run the pub and are very proud of being the only pub for 30 miles which is both in the CAMRA 'Good Pub Food Guide' and 'The Good Beer Guide' and of its reputation for having a friendly, welcoming atmosphere. B & B accommodation is also available.

King William IV, Kirksanton, Millom, Cumbria. Tel: 01229 772009

HAVERIGG. In the centre of this small coastal village is **GILLGARTH**, an old coaching station which provided food and shelter to travellers when the building was owned by the Lords of nearby Millom Castle. Gillgarth is still offering the traveller a warm welcome today, though now with view to the needs of the 20th century and is ETB registered. Owned and run by Margaret Barnes, this bed and breakfast establishment has a warm and homely atmosphere with many extra facilities that make your stay so much more enjoyable. Evening meals are available and special diets can be catered for, both by prior arrangement. In this private location, set in a large garden, there is much to offer the traveller and holidaymaker.

Gillgarth, Caton Street, Haverigg, Millom Tel: 01229 772531

The area of coastline between Kirksanton and the ancient Roman port of Ravenglass is the only part of a National Park to come in contact with the sea.

RAVENGLASS, lies on the estuary of three rivers - the Esk, the Mite and the Irt. Because of its sheltered position, Ravenglass became an important naval-base for the Romans in the 2nd century. It was a supply point for the military zone around Hadrian's Wall. Except for a remarkable **BATH HOUSE**, little remains now of their large fort of **'GLANNAVENTRA'** on the cliffs above the village. The Bath House is an impressive building and one of the best surviving Roman structures in England, with walls over 12ft high.

In the 18th century Ravenglass was a base for smugglers bringing contraband in from coastal ships - tobacco and French brandy. Today the estuary has silted up but there are still scores of small boats and the village is a charming resort, full of atmosphere. The layout has changed little since the 16th century. The main street is paved with sea-pebbles and leads up from a shingle beach. Once, iron-ore was brought to the estuary by narrow-gauge railway from the mines near Boot, in Eskdale, about eight miles away.

In the centre of Ravenglass lies the **PENNINGTON ARMS** hotel. This traditional hotel, owned and run by Yvonne and Dave Stewart, is decorated and furnished in a manner in keeping with the period of the hotel and there are open fires in the reception rooms to bring cheer to the chilly days and evenings. The intimate restaurant specialises in seafood and there are also some mouth-watering Italian dishes to tempt you. Children and pets, by arrangement, are welcome and this is an ideal place to stay on the Cumbrian coast, with the estuary and the famous Ravenglass railway on a few minutes stroll from the hotel.

Pennington Arms, Main Street, Ravenglass Tel: 01229 71722

THE RAVENGLASS AND ESKDALE RAILWAY, which runs for seven miles up the lovely Mite and Esk River valleys, was first opened to passengers in 1876 since when it has survived several threats of extinction. In 1915 it was converted from 3ft-gauge track to a new miniature 15in-gauge and carried passengers and freight - which later included granite - between Ravenglass and Dalegarth. However, towards the end of the 1950s, the closure of the granite quarries seemed to spell disaster for 'T'laal Ratty' (as the railway is affectionately known). At the auction of the railway in 1960 a band of enthusiasts outbid the scrap-dealers and a company was formed to keep the little railway running.

Today there are twelve locomotives, both steam and diesel, and 300,000 people a year come from all over the world to ride on 'T'laal Ratty' and enjoy the splendour of Eskdale. It is still the best way to explore Mitedale and Eskdale, enchanting both young and old.

At Ravenglass there is a fascinating small **MUSEUM OF IRON ORE MINING** and the history of the line. The station has a souvenir shop and refreshment room. The 100-year old British Railways station building was converted into **THE RATTY ARMS**, the railway's own pub.

MUNCASTER MILL, a mile or so up the River Mite, is reached by Eskdale trains and has working machinery dating from the late 18th century. A mill has stood here since the 15th century, though the present building only dates from around 1700. It was carefully restored by the Railway Company in 1976-8 and is powered by a great, overshot waterwheel. It still produces a wide variety of stone-ground, wholemeal flours.

A mile or so east of Ravenglass stands **MUNCASTER CASTLE**, an impressive castellated mansion which has been owned by the Pennington family since 1208. It has grown from the original Pele Tower built on Roman foundations to the impressive structure that can be seen today. Outstanding features are the Great Hall, Salvin's octagonal library and the drawing room with its barrel ceiling. Muncaster contains many treasures including beautiful furniture, tapestries, silver and porcelain. In 1464, King Henry VI sheltered here from his enemies after losing the Battle of Hexham. In gratitude, he left his glass enamelled drinking bowl, now known as the Luck of Muncaster, saying that the Pennington family will live at the Castle as long as the bowl remains unbroken. The woodland gardens cover 77 acres and command spectacular views of the Lakeland Fells. From mid-March to June, the famous rhododendrons, azaleas and camellias are at their best.

The grounds also contain a fascinating **OWL CENTRE**. Here, visitors can meet the birds daily at 2.30pm (April to end October) when a talk is given on the work of the centre, and weather permitting, the owls display their flying skills. The gardens and owl centre are open daily throughout the year; castle open afternoons end-March to end-October (closed Mondays).

Muncaster Castle, Nr Ravenglass 01229 717614

IRTON. **IRTON HALL** lies in this ancient village, just two miles from Drigg in Eskdale. The village and the Hall are, historically, closely linked and there has been a lord of the manor at the Hall since the 14th century. Unfortunately over the years the building has been altered greatly but its original fortress-dwelling purpose is reflected in its strong defensive position, where on two sides the ground descends steeply down to the Frithgill and the Irt. Now owned and run by Harry and Lisa Lingard and family, the Hall and its extensive grounds offer self catering accommodation in five separate houses.

A well equipped playground and petting zoo are available for the use of younger visitors, there are bicycles available and Mrs Lingard is happy to arrange for a professional baby sitter in the evenings. This is a super place for a family holiday with plenty of fine countryside and history right on the doorstep. 5 Keys Highly Commended.

Irton Hall, Irton, Holmrook, Eskdale Tel: 019467 26040

BOOT lies at the eastern end of the Ravenglass and Eskdale Railway and is a wonderful place to visit whether arriving by train or car. It is a gentle walk from the station at Eskdale, and is a delightful village, with its pub, post office, museum watermill and nearby St Catherine's Church in its riverside setting.

Housed in a converted barn in the attractive village of Boot is **FOLD END GALLERY**. The gallery has been in existence since 1973 and exhibits the works of over one hundred craftspeople, all to the highest standard. As well as a large selection of original watercolours, etchings and pastels, the gallery displays welded steel sculptures by Gordon Griffiths and bronzes and wood carvings by Robert Campbell. There is also a wide choice of hand blown glass, and handmade ceramics from over thirty different potters. Exquisite amber, enamel, haematite, slate and silver jewellery is regularly stocked. Open Tuesdays to Sundays, 10am to 5.30pm.(Closed Mondays)

Fold End Gallery, Boot, Eskdale, Cumbria CA19 1TE Tel: 019467 23213

Popular with walkers and tourists alike, the **BROOK HOUSE**

HOTEL, which nestles in this tiny village, at the foot of Scafell, enjoys panoramic views of the surrounding countryside and offers B & B accommodation of a high standard. This Victorian hotel has recently been refurbished and great care has been taken to preserve its character. The atmosphere is warm, friendly and relaxed. You will find that all eight bedrooms have en-suite facilities and are comfortable and well appointed with bath and showers, TV, Coffee and tea making facilities.

First class home cooking by their excellent chefs and fine wines are served in the restaurant with a log fire where you can enjoy ales and good malt whisky.

Pat and Eddie, the owners, have worked hard to build up the fine reputation that this hotel now deservedly enjoys.for peace and tranquility a walkers paradise.

ETB 3 Crowns commended

Brook House Hotel, Boot, Eskdale, Cumbria. Tel 019467 23288

GOSFORTH, further north along the A595 is famous for its 15ft-high **VIKING CROSS** which towers above the huddled gravestones in a peaceful churchyard. Carved from red sandstone and clearly influenced by both Christian and pagan tradition, it depicts the crucifixion, the deeds of Norse gods and 'Yggdrasil', the World Ash Tree that Norsemen believed supported the universe.

ST MARY'S is built on the site of an earlier Norman church and contains several other ancient relics. The Chinese Bell on the western window-sill of the church was captured in 1841 at Anunkry, a fort on the River Canton. Look out, too, for the delightful carved faces on the chancel arch and a cork tree planted in 1833.

NETHER WASDALE is a tiny, tranquil Cumbrian village nestling at the foot of Wasdale, just east of Gosforth. Situated near here, at the foot of **GREAT GABLE**, just past the Parish Church of St Olaf in Wasdale Head, lies **BURNTHWAITE FARM**. Still a working farm, Audrey Buchanan offers bed and breakfast accommodation in the farmhouse in six bedrooms with an evening meal by arrangement. A warm and friendly establishment this is an ideal place for discovering the delights of the surrounding lakes and fells. As well as offering accommodation at the farmhouse, Audrey lets Burnthwaite Cottage, a charming building, which sleeps five, with all the accommodation at ground level. With a fully equipped kitchen, the cottage has two bedrooms, a bathroom and a sitting room. In the heart of some of England's most majestic countryside, this is a wonderful spot for a family holiday.

Burnthwaite, Wasdale Head, Gosforth Tel: 019467 26242

EGREMONT is dominated by its **NORMAN CASTLE** standing high above the town, overlooking the lovely River Ehen to the south and the market place to the north. The castle was built between 1130 and 1140 by William de Meschines on the site of a former Danish fortification. The most complete part still standing is a Norman arch that once guarded the drawbridge entrance. Nearby is an unusual four-sided sundial and the stump of the old market-cross dating from the early 13th century.

Wordsworth's poem, 'The Horn of Egremont Castle', is based on a local legend from the Middle Ages. It is said that a great horn hanging in the castle could only be blown by the rightful lord. In the 13th century Hubert de Lucy arranged to have the rightful lord, his brother Eustace, murdered so that he could claim his title. The plot misfired and during the celebration feast to mark Hubert's inheritance, Eustace returned to blow the horn. Hubert, wisely, fled to a monastery.

Egremont's prosperity was based on the good quality of its local iron-ore. Today it still retains a strong 19th century air with its simple, colour-washed houses opening directly onto the street. Wander down the wide, tree-lined main street towards the Parish Church of St Mary and St Michael, a superb example of Victorian Gothic architecture.

In September every year the town celebrates its **CRAB FAIR**. The fair dates from the 13th century when crab-apples were distributed to bystanders. Now Worcestershire apples are thrown from a lorry which drives down the main street. The fair is usually celebrated with traditional sports which include wrestling and hound-trailing. The highlight is **THE WORLD GURNING CHAMPIONSHIP** in which each 'gurner' puts his head through a horse collar and pulls an ugly face - the ugliest being declared the winner!

There are some particularly fine walks from Egremont, over the fells, passing through small villages like Wilton and Haile.

HAILE stands on a hill overlooking a simple, modern church which has ancient stones incorporated into the fabric, some with Roman inscriptions. A fine avenue of beech trees leads to a stone gate-house and archway through which can be seen 16th century **HAILE HALL**.

CALDER BRIDGE is a nearby small, grey, 19th century settlement where **CALDER ABBEY**, is linked to the village by an attractive footpath. It was founded by monks of Savigny in 1134 but amalgamated with the Cistercians of Furness Abbey when it was ransacked by the Scots a few years later. After the Dissolution the monastery buildings lapsed slowly into the present-day romantic ruin. Part of the tower and west doorway remain, with some of the chancel and transept, but sadly these are unsafe and have to be viewed from the road.

THE RIVER CALDER rises on **CAW FELL** south of Ennerdale Water. **MONK'S BRIDGE**, the oldest packhorse bridge in Cumbria, was built for the monks and has no parapets in order to accommodate the panniers, or sacks, of the loaded pack-horses.

St Bees Head, a red sandstone bluff, forms one of the most dramatic natural features along the entire coast of North-west England. It is four miles of towering, precipitous cliffs of 'St Bees Sandstone', the red rock which is so characteristic of Cumbria. Far out to sea, on the horizon, can be seen the grey shadow of the Isle of Man, and on a clear day, the shimmering outline of the Irish coast. From St Bees Head the 190 mile Coast to Coast Walk starts on its long journey across the Pennines to Robin Hood's Bay on the East Coast.

Long before the first lighthouse was built in 1822, there was a beacon on the headland to warn and guide passing ships away from the rocks. The present lighthouse dates from 1866-7, built after an earlier one was destroyed by fire. St Bees Head is now an important Nature Reserve and the cliffs are crowded with guillemots, razorbills, kittiwakes, gulls, gannets and skuas and you'll find Observation and Information Points all along the headland. There is a superb walk of about eight miles along the coastal footpath around the headland from St Bees to Whitehaven.

ST. BEES, a short walk from the headland is a small village which lies huddled in a deep, slanting bowl in the cliffs, fringed by a shingle beach. The village is a delightful place to explore, with its main street winding up the hillside between old farms and cottages. It derives its name from 'St Bega', daughter of an Irish king who, on the day she was meant to marry a Norse prince, was miraculously transported by an angel to the Cumbrian coast. According to legend, on Midsummer Night's Eve, St Bega asked the pagan Lord Egremont for some land on which to found a Nunnery. Cunningly, he promised her only as much land as was covered by snow the following morning. But on Midsummer's Day, three square miles of land were blanketed white with snow and here she founded her Priory.

Soon after, however, forced to flee from her rejected suitor, she took refuge in the King of Northumbria's court; there she helped to found Whitby Abbey. The Priory at St Bees grew in size and importance until it was destroyed by the Danes in the 10th century. The Benedictines later re-established the Priory in 1129. **THE PRIORY CHURCH OF ST. MARY'S AND ST. BEGA** is all that is now left but, although it has been substantially altered, there is still a magnificent Norman arch. Look out for the pre-Conquest, carved **BEOWULF STONE** on a lintel between the Church and the Vicarage, showing St Michael killing a dragon.

Close by the Church are the charming **ABBEY COTTAGES** and **ST BEES SCHOOL** with its handsome clock-tower. The school was founded in 1583 by Edmund Grindal, Archbishop of Canterbury under Elizabeth I, and the son of a local farmer. The original red sandstone quadrangle bears his coat-of-arms and the bridge he gave to the village is still in use.

Within a few minutes stroll of the beach at St Bees and close to the centre of the village lies **TOMLIN GUEST HOUSE**. Owned and run by Irene and David Whitehead, bed and breakfast accommodation is offered in four rooms in this quiet and friendly establishment.

Tomlin Guest House, 1 Tomlin House, Beach Road, St Bees
Tel: 01946 822284

Excellent bed & breakfast accomodation can be found near St Bees at the unusually named **KHANDHALLA**, a peaceful country house set in a beautiful 2 acre walled garden and orchard. Close to the village, together with its station and amenities, this is the ideal choice for a holiday or short break spent exploring this fascinating area. Nine comfortable, tastefully furnished rooms are available, three have en-suite bathroom facilities. The hosts, Tom and Dinah, are very friendly and you can be sure of the warmest welcome.

Khandahalla B & B, High House Road, St. Bees, Cumbria.
Tel: 01946 822377

The **HUNDAY MANOR HOTEL**, originally an 18th century manor house, can be found just off the **A595** approaching Whitehaven from the

A66. This small hotel has a friendly, welcoming atmosphere together with everything that you would expect from a modern hotel of this type. It is set in wooded grounds on the northern edge of the Lake District and is the ideal base, not only for the Lakes, but also for Cockermouth, Workington, Whitehaven and Keswick.

All 12 bedrooms are well furnished and equipped, and have en-suite bathrooms. A choice of excellent food is served in the restaurant, diners can choose from the first-class a la carte or table d'hote menus. Meals are served in the elegant old dining room or the spacious garden room.

This lovely hotel provides a warm welcome, good food, comfortable rooms and, above all, good service.

Hunday Manor Hotel, Hunday, Workington. Tel: 01900 61798

WHITEHAVEN was established in the 12th century as a harbour for use by the monks of nearby St Bees Priory, but most of the town was developed by the Lowther family to carry coal from their mines near the coast. In the mid-18th century Whitehaven was an important port, its trade based on coal and other cargo business. It was a larger port than Liverpool at that time and ranked only third in national importance after London and Bristol. It imported tobacco from Virginia, exported coal to Ireland and saw the emigration of settlers to the New World. However, in the days of large iron-steamships, its shallow draught halted expansion and the port declined in favour of Liverpool and Southampton. For that reason much of the attractive harbour area - now full of pleasure craft and fishing smacks - and older parts of the town remain unchanged.

There used to be two parish churches in Whitehaven - St James and St Nicholas. **ST. JAMES** stands on a hill at the top of Queen Street, was built between 1752-3 and contains one of the finest Georgian church interiors in Cumbria. **ST. NICHOLAS**, on Lowther Street, was largely destroyed by fire in 1971 but an attractive garden now surrounds the ruins. A plaque marks the burial place of Mildred Warner Gale, better known as George Washington's grandmother, who died in 1700 and is buried here.

There is a fascinating Town 'Walkabout' Trail and a Nature Trail around **TOM HURD ROCK**, above the town. Leaflets can be obtained from the Information Centre in **ST NICHOLAS TOWER** in Lowther Street. There is also the particularly interesting **WHITEHAVEN MUSEUM AND ART GALLERY**. The Museum deals with the history of the whole of Copeland (the District of Cumbria in which Whitehaven lies) with special emphasis on its mining and maritime history. The displays reflect the many aspects of this harbour-borough with a collection which includes paintings, locally made pottery, ship models and navigational instruments, miners lamps and surveying equipment. The Beilby 'Slavery' Goblet, part of the museum's collection, is one of the masterpieces of English glass-making and is probably the finest example of its kind in existence.

The town is interesting in other ways. It still has a 'grid iron' pattern of streets dating back to the 17th century, a layout that can claim to be the first planned town in Britain. Many of the fine Georgian buildings in the centre have been restored and Lowther Street is a particularly impressive thoroughfare. Also of note is the harbour pier built by canal engineer, John Rennie, and considered to be one of the finest in Britain.

CLEATOR MOOR. Touring Cumbria and the Lake District by caravan is always popular, although good camp sites handy for the lakes are not always easy to find. Perhaps the finest camp site in this area is **THE CLEATOR MOOR CARAVAN PARK** which is run by the Cleator Moor Reacreation and Leisure Trust and is situated on Quarry Road, Cleator Moor. This site has ample space for sixty touring caravans, and more besides for tenting enthusiasts. The site's facilities are truly excellent, it boasts fully equipped shower blocks, laundry rooms, a superb all-weather astro-turf football pitch, an indoor flat-green bowling centre with four rinks and a lounge/bar equipped to receive Sky Television. It would be difficult to find another campsite in the area that could match these facilities and location or provide such a lovely setting for the perfect camping holiday.

Cleator Moor Caravan Park, Quarry Road, Cleator Moor. Tel:01946 815419

Ornate Medieval Doorway at St. Bees Priory

Boot Village

CHAPTER NINE

The North Cumbrian Coast

Kirkstile Inn and Church, Loweswater

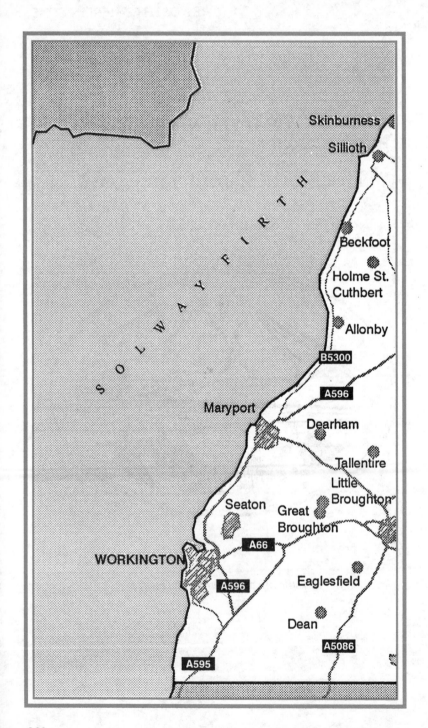

Skinburness

Sillioth

Beckfoot

Holme St.
Cuthbert

Allonby

B5300

A596

Maryport

Dearham

Tallentire

Little
Broughton

Seaton
Great
Broughton

A66

WORKINGTON

A596

Eaglesfield

Dean

A5086

A595

SOLWAY FIRTH

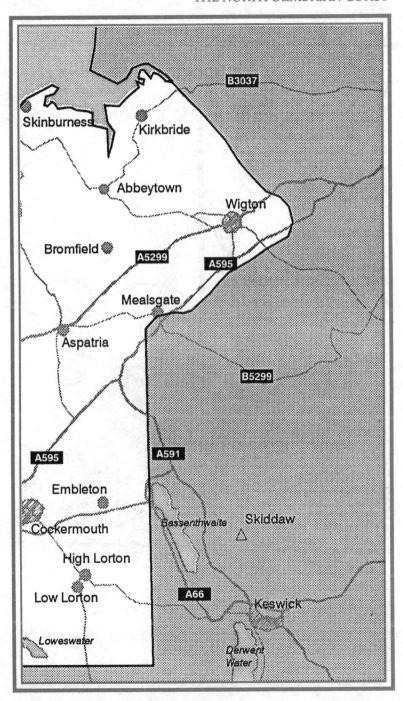

VIC 96, Naval Supply Ship, Elizabeth Dock, Maryport

CHAPTER NINE

The North Cumbrian Coast

WORKINGTON, the largest town on the Cumbrian coast, stands at the mouth of the River Derwent on the site of a former Roman fort of 'Gabrosentum'. Its prosperity was founded on three great Cumbrian industries - coal, iron and shipping. As early as 1650 coal was being mined here and, by the end of the 18th century, Workington was a major port exporting coal as well as smelting iron-ore. Many of the underground coal seams extended far out to sea. In later years Workington was famous for its fine-quality steel, and it is still the place in Britain where most railway lines are manufactured. It also has a national reputation for the buses and lorries that are built just outside the town.

WORKINGTON HALL was the Curwen family seat for over 600 years and has a fascinating history. Originally built up around a 14th century Peel Tower, the Hall was developed over the years with extensive alterations being made in the eighteenth century by the then lord of the manor, John Christian Curwen. Now a stabilised ruin, there are commemorative plaques which give a taste of the Hall's history. The most famous visitor to the Hall was Mary Queen of Scots who sought refuge here when she fled from Scotland in 1558. She stayed for a few days during which time she wrote a letter to her cousin Queen Elizabeth I seeking advice and assistance. The letter is now housed in the British Museum.

Workington Hall, Workington 01900 604351

THE HELENA THOMPSON MUSEUM situated on Park End Road is fascinating place to visit with its displays telling the story of

Workington's coal mining, shipbuilding, iron and steel industries for which the town became internationally renowned. The Georgian Room gives an insight into the variety of decorative styles which were popular between 1714 and 1830, with displays of beautiful cut-glass tableware, porcelain from China, and period pieces of furniture.

Helena Thompson Museum

Bequeathed to the town by Miss Helena Thompson, M.B.E., J.P., the museum was opened in 1949 and contains some of her own family heirlooms. One particularly interesting museum exhibit is the Clifton Dish, a locally produced 18th century piece of slipware pottery and displays show the links between this local industry and the famous Staffordshire pottery families.

Helena Thompson Museum, Park End Road, Workington
Tel: 01900 604351

The Westlands Hotel

THE WESTLANDS HOTEL in Workington has an excellent reputation for providing a high standard of friendly service. The hotel is situated just one and a half miles from Workington's town centre on

Branthwaite Road and is ideally situated as a base for a business stay or for exploring all of the places featured in this chapter.

The hotel has recently been completely refurbished and now boasts eighty-two well equipped rooms, all of which have TV, drinks making facilities, hairdryer, trouser press and en-suite bathroom.

In addition there is an excellent restaurant, which serves the finest quality dishes using the very freshest local produce wherever possible.

The hotel has deservedly been awarded an RAC 3 Star rating.

The Westlands Hotel, Branthwaite Road, Workington.
Tel: 01900 604544 Fax: 01900 68830

DEAN, some six miles east of Workington, is a charming village full of old houses and farms. The churchyard is entered through a lychgate and outside the church is an ancient preaching-cross probably dating from the 12th century. Three original 15th-century gargoyles, one face downwards, decorate the south wall.

Dean is sign posted off the A5086 Cockermouth to Egremont road and is the picturesque location of **THE ROYAL YEW**, a charming country pub run by Alistair Chalmers. Open seven days a week, this cosy, welcoming establishment is renowned locally for its superb bar food and justly so. The menu is varied and imaginative, with best selling dishes such as Old Peculiar Pie, a home-made steak and mushroom pie, and Pavlova the most popular dessert. There are a wide range of steak dishes as well as other main courses, and a children's menu. All are very reasonably priced, and with the accompanying wine list, which includes wines from all over the world, The Royal Yew makes the perfect venue for lunch or dinner.

The Royal Yew, Dean, Workington. Tel: 01946 861342

ENNERDALE, southwards of Dean, is truly a hidden place. It is tranquil and quiet offering lake shores, river banks, valley paths and forest tracks which together offer a tremendous variety of walks suitable for all ages and capabilities. Other activities available include fishing, canoeing, bird watching and pony trekking. Wainwright's coast to coast walk runs the whole length of Ennerdale and the general consensus is that this section is by far the most beautiful.

MARYPORT, along the coast north of Workington, is a town rich in interest. The old part is full of narrow streets, neo-classical, Georgian architecture and quaint, picturesque neeks which contrast with sudden, surprising views of the sea.

Modern Maryport dates from the 18th century when Humphrey Senhouse, a local landowner, developed the harbour to export coal from his mines, naming the new port after his wife, Mary. Over the next century it became a busy port as well as a ship-building centre, boats having to be launched broadside because of the narrowness of the harbour channel. The town declined, along with the mining industry, from the 1930's onwards. However, it is now enjoying a well-earned revival, with newly-restored Georgian quaysides, steep cobbled streets, clifftop paths, sandy beaches and a harbour full of fishing boats and colourful pleasure craft.

Maryport lies on the Solway Firth just 27 miles from Carlisle. The town's extensive maritime history is preserved in the vast array of objects, pictures and models on display at **MARYPORT MARITIME MUSEUM**, a fascinating place to visit.

Maryport Maritime Museum, Maryport 01900 604351

Just down the road from the Maritime Museum, at Elizabeth Dock, you will find **MARYPORT STEAMSHIPS**, where you can learn all about Maryport's shipbuilding industry. Take a tour round the VIC96 where you can have a go at raising and lowering sails on a Brigantine model, learn how to tie ship's knots and even climb into a sailor's hammock! Step onto The Flying Buzzard and find yourself back in the 1950's with a running commentary bringing to life this former pride of the Clyde Shipping Company's Tug Fleet. Here you can visit the engine room and discover how The Buzzard worked and why she sank.

Maryport Steamships, Elizabeth Dock, Maryport 01900 604351

DEARHAM, about two miles inland from Maryport, though not a pretty village, has a very beautiful church with open countryside on three sides. The chancel is 13th century and there is a fortress tower built for the protection of men and beasts during the Border raids. Standing 4ft high is the Adam Stone, dating from AD900, depicting the fall of man, with Adam and Eve hand in hand above a serpent. There is also an ancient font carved with mythological beasts, a Kenneth Cross showing the legend of the 6th-century hermit brought up by seagulls, and a magnificent wheel-head cross, 5ft 4in high, carved with 'Yggdrasil', the Norse Tree of the Universe.

Enjoying a quiet location in the centre of Dearham, you will find **THE OLD MILL**, so named because part of the building dates back to the 17th century and used to operate as a corn mill. The interior is particularly attractive with unusual painted panes of glass throughout, which feature brightly coloured flowers, butterflies and birds. Run by Angela Greenwood, this charming pub offers such delights as Local Trout grilled with Almonds, Spinach and Mushroom Lasagne and Chewy Fudge Brownie Cheesecake. The Old Mill also provides accommodation in seven tastefully co-ordinated guest rooms, two of which are en-suite and all with TV and hot drinks facilities.

The Old Mill Inn and Restaurant, Dearham, Nr Maryport.
Tel: 01900 813184

BRIDEKIRK, just north of Cockermouth, is well worth visiting for its church which contains one of the finest pieces of Norman sculpture in the country, a carved font with runic inscription and a mass of detailed embellishments. It dates from the 12th century and the runic inscription states it was made by 'Richard'. He is shown on one side with a chisel and mallet. Not only is this a superb example of early English craftsmanship, but it is exceedingly rare to find a signed work. Ancient tombstones stand round the walls of the cruciform church and inside it has unusual reredos (a wall behind the altar) of fleur-de-lys patterned tiles.

LITTLE BROUGHTON and GREAT BROUGHTON on the River Derwent, south-east of Maryport, were communities involved in weaving and pipemaking.

Above the banks of the River Derwent with rolling views over the

Lakeland Fells to the slopes of Skiddaw, **BROUGHTON CRAGGS HOTEL** with its own extensive grounds and gardens offers visitors the opportunity to enjoy special hospitality and first class cuisine in a tranquil setting. A wide variety of activities are available and include:

Fellwalking, rockclimbing, windsurfing, canoeing, sailing, golf, clay pigeon shooting and horse riding. The 14 stylish bedrooms are all en suite and are equipped with telephones, colour televisions and tea and coffee making facilities. Follow the A66 from Cockermouth heading to Workington, take the first turning on the right to Great Broughton, cross the River Derwent - the hotel is at the top of the hill.

Broughton Craggs Hotel, Great Broughton, Nr. Cockermouth, Cumbria.
Tel: 01900 824400

Further downstream is CAMERTON, whose old, grassed-over slag-heaps are the only evidence of its coal-mining origins. Camerton is set in a particularly lovely section of the wooded Derwent Valley with the panorama of the Lakeland Fells as a backcloth. In the small and ancient church stands a memorial statue of 'Black Tom', the famous warrior Thomas Curwein, who died in 1500.

EAGLESFIELD was the birthplace of Robert Eaglesfield, who became confessor to Queen Philippa, Edward III's Queen. He was also the founder of Queen's College, Oxford where he was buried in 1349. More famous is John Dalton who was born here in 1766. The son of Quaker parents, Dalton was one of the most brilliant scientists, naturalists, and mathematicians of his age and was the originator of atomic theory. A memorial now marks his house. He taught at the village school at the age of 12, before going to Manchester to follow his remarkable scientific career.

A fine base for a walking holiday in the Lake District is to be found near Eaglesfield. **BENT ASH FARM** is a working farm with a friendly atmosphere offering Bed and Breakfast accomodation. The farm is situated in beautiful countryside overlooking the Lakeland Fells and in the distance you can see as far as the Scottish Mountains beyond the Solway Firth. Four tastefully decorated, oak panelled rooms are available, two of these are equipped with en-suite bathrooms. In the morning you will enjoy a hearty home cooked English breakfast - a perfect start for a day spent walking in the Fells. Packed lunches and evening meals are available on request. Evening tea and cakes at 10pm. are included in terms. A no-smoking home.

Bent Ash Farm, Eaglesfield, Nr Cockermouth, Cumbria CA13 0SR
Tel:01900 822387

COCKERMOUTH is a Cumbrian market-town which has retained its unspoiled character, less overrun by tourists than its neighbours to the west. There are pleasant shops and restaurants along a busy main street set against a majestic backdrop of fells. Wordsworth was born here and his old home in Main Street, which has been at various times a shop, a cobbler's and a tearoom, was the National Trust's first Information Centre, a function which it still retains. Now known as the **WORDSWORTH HOUSE**, it was built in 1745 and retains its original staircase, fireplace and fine plaster ceilings. There are some personal effects of the poet and you can visit his childhood garden.

Another famous son of Cockermouth was Fletcher Christian, the man who led the mutiny on 'The Bounty'. He was born in 1764, at Moorland Close, a farm about a mile south of the town, and attended the same school as Wordsworth.

After several years of showing their work in galleries and exhibitions in the North, Rolf and Deborah Parker moved to Cockermouth in 1994 to open their own gallery in South Street. **SKYLARK STUDIO** is a small gallery displaying the work of local artist Rolf Parker whose studio is above the sales area. Here he divides his time between painting in watercolours and producing etchings of the local landscape and street scenes. Deborah Parker makes a wide range of fashion jewellery including original designs in enamel on copper. The shop stocks an exclusive range of high quality British made crafts including decorative ceramics, functional pottery, handmade glass and cards.

Skylark Studio, 9 South Street, Cockermouth. Tel 01900 823521

There has been a livestock auction in Cockermouth since 1873 , a part of the rural scene in the Lakes which tourists do not often see.

An integral part of this slice of Cumbrian life is **THE FAIRFIELD RESTAURANT** which is located adjacent to the Livestock market . Grace and John Hadden run the restaurant which is in the auction buildings complex and provide customers with good wholesome food which is prepared and served by them using local produce. If you do not want a full meal, bar snacks are available in the bar. The restaurant which is open every day except Tuesday, is licensed and there is ample parking with coach parties catered for by prior arrangement.

The Fairfield Restaurant Station St. Cockermouth. Tel: 01900 822037

COCKERMOUTH CASTLE dates from the 13th and 14th centuries but is not open to the public. Part of it was built with material from the Roman Fort 'Derventio', at Papcastle, immediately north-west of Cockermouth. It has had an eventful history; it was besieged by Robert the Bruce and saw action in both the Wars of the Roses and the Civil War.

Dating, in part, from 1752, **ROSE COTTAGE GUEST HOUSE**, on the outskirts of Cockermouth was originally an Inn and for many years a 'Tuck Shop' to the local Grammar School! For the past twenty years it has successfully been run as a guest house under the experienced ownership of resident proprietors John and Susan Graham. Most of the nine bedrooms are en-suite and all have central heating, colour TV, tea and coffee making facilities and are comfortably furnished. An excellent full English breakfast is provided and dinner is available every evening except Sunday. A fine range of wines is also available. Situated in Cockermouth on the right hand side of Lorton road heading towards Lorton and Buttermere.

Rose Cottage Guest House, Lorton Road, Cockermouth, Cumbria.
Tel: 01900 822189

For an insight into West Cumbrian life and history, be sure to visit the **LAKELAND SHEEP AND WOOL CENTRE** on the outskirts of Cockermouth at the junction of the **A66** and **A5086**. This recently opened visitor centre houses fascinating exhibitions and has daily sheep shearing and shepherding demonstrations throughout the summer.

Lakeland Sheep and Wool Centr

Within the show, which takes place four times daily and features nineteen different breeds of live sheep, some of them very rare. The

213

centre has a gift shop which, unsurprisingly, specialises in high quality pure wool products, ideal for presents.

This is a handy location for exploring the area, so you may wish to spend a few nights in the **SHEPHERDS HOTEL** which is also part of the centre. The building is only one year old and consequently is very light and spacious. The rooms are very comfortable and well equipped, all have en-suite bathrooms. You will enjoy the fine food which is served in the restaurant, particularly worthy of note is the Farmhouse Fayre bar menu.

The standard of service is excellent and you can be assured of an enjoyable stay at this fine hotel.

The Shepherds Hotel & Lakeland Sheep and Wool Centre, Egremont Road, Cockermouth. Tel/fax: 01900 822673

Heading out of Cockermouth towards Lorton and Buttermere you will find the **HUNDITH HILL HOTEL**. This superb hotel is set in the loveliest of gardens and woodland and offers the very finest in accommodation and food.

Hundith Hill Hotel, Lorton Vale, Cockermouth, Cumbria. Tel: 01900 822050, Fax: 0900 828215

If you are looking for holiday accommodation close to Cockermouth then the **VIOLET BANK CARAVAN PARK** is worth seeking out. Here the gently sloping grasslands afford a stunning panoramic view of Lorton Valley and the majestic Buttermere Fells. A superb place to relax whilst surrounded by breathtaking scenery. The majority of the static caravans and holiday homes here are privately owned, however two of the luxury holiday homes can be let for weekend breaks or longer holidays. If you are energetic you can partcipate in one of the many country pusuits which are available nearby; these include forestry and nature trails, climbing, fishing, swimming, squash, pony trekking and, of course, fell walking. Approach by way of the A5292 Lorton Road from

Cockermouth town centre. Turn right into Vicarage Lane, left into Simonscales Lane.

Violet Bank Caravan Park, Simonscales Lane, Cockermouth.
Tel: 01900 822169

MOCKERKIN. Offering accommodation for up to ten people, the group of five picturesque self-catering cottages at Mockerkin, near Cockermouth make a first rate centre for walking holidays. The **BROADINGS HOLIDAY COTTAGES** are furnished to the very highest standard and have inglenook log fires and luxurious Jacuzzis. The owner of the cottages, Mrs Christine Greening, also runs a working dairy farm and visitors are encouraged to take a look around. The cottages are set in the finest countryside only two miles from Loweswater, Crummock and Buttermere and enjoy lovely views as far as the Scottish mountain ranges on the far side of the Solway Firth. English Tourist Board 4 keys highly recommended.

Broadings Holiday Cottages, Mockerkin, Nr Cockermouth, Cumbria
Tel: 01946 861672

Two miles from Cockermouth lies the picturesque village of **TALLENTIRE** where you will find a lovely 17th century pub, **THE BUSH INN**. Pretty hanging baskets adorn the entrance and there is a warm friendly atmosphere inside where you will soon find yourself feeling at home as you have a drink and a chat with the locals. Host Alan Wilkie provides excellent bar meals six days a week, both at lunchtime and in the evening. The menu is extensive and varied with something to suit every palate, including a wide range of vegetarian dishes and an above average children's menu. With the large food portions and nice selection of accompanying wines, a meal at the Bush Inn is a real treat.

The Bush Inn, Tallentire, Cockermouth. Tel: 01900 823707

LOWESWATER, which can only be reached by narrow lanes, is one of the smaller of the lakes, in an enchanting fell-side and forest setting. From Cockermouth, take the B5292 and at Lorton, the B5289, turning off to Brackenthwaite, after which you will come to Loweswater village. A public bridleway which takes you around the far side of the lake, whose name, appropriately, means 'leafy lake'. You can return along a quiet lane at the far side and there is a car park near Waterend.

North of Loweswater is one of the quietest and least-known parts of the Lake District National Park, a group of low fells through which there are few roads or even paths, summits such as Fellbarrow, Smithy Fell, Sourfoot Fell. The little river Cocker divides this group from the Lorton Fells, further east, forming the Beautiful Vale of Lorton.

LORTON is a village in two parts. **LOW LORTON** has a pele tower and **LORTON HALL** is reputed to be haunted by a woman carrying a lighted candle. There are also two priest holes. The Scottish King Malcolm III (1057-93) stayed at the Hall with his Queen on a visit to the southern part of his Kingdom of Strathclyde - at that time part of Scotland.

HIGH LORTON, about half a mile away, has a village hall known as Yew Tree Hall where the Quaker George Fox preached to Cromwell's soldiers. The yew tree that stands nearby inspired Wordsworth's famous poem which begins, *'There is a yew tree, pride of Lorton Vale....'.*

From High Lorton a steep road travels east through the thickly forested Lorton Fells, over the Whinlatter Pass to Braithwaite, to Derwent Water and Bassenthwaite Lake.

From Lorton and beyond Brackenthwaite, the B5289 skirts the edge of Crummock Water and continues to BUTTERMERE. The walk around Buttermere gives superb views. One of the great scandals of the 19th century involved Mary Robinson, the Beauty of Buttermere, who thought she had married the Earl of Hopetoun's brother, only to discover that in fact her husband was a bankrupt imposter. He was hanged and she later married a local farmer.

The north-west corner of Cumbria, overlooking the Solway Firth dividing England and Scotland, is perhaps the least-known part of this beautiful county. And yet it is an area rich in heritage, with a network of quiet country lanes, little-frequented villages, old ports and seaside resorts along a coast which is full of atmosphere.

WIGTON has, for centuries, been the centre of the business and social life of the Solway coast and plain, its prosperity based on the weaving of cotton and linen. It has enjoyed the benefits of a Royal Charter since 1262 and a market is still held on Tuesdays. Today most of the old town is a Conservation Area and if you look carefully along the Main Street, you can see how the upper storeys of the houses have survived in an almost unaltered state. On street corners, metal guards to prevent heavy horse-drawn waggons damaging the walls, can still be seen.

BASKETS AND BUNCHES is a delightful gift shop and florist on Wigton's High Street. Mary, the owner, dries fresh flowers and produces beautiful arrangements which are displayed for sale in the shop. In addition a wide range of basketware, candles and candle holders, aromatherapy oils and burners, soaps, pictures and vases are on sale. Make sure that you pop in for a browse, there are plenty of interesting things to look at and choose from, you won't be stuck for ideas for that special gift.

Baskets and Bunches, 15 High Street, Wigton. Tel: 016973 45768

The Memorial Fountain, Wigton

Not to be missed is the magnificent **MEMORIAL FOUNTAIN** in the Market Place, its gilded, floriate panels set against Shap granite and surmounted with a golden cross. It was erected in 1872 by George Moore, a 19th-century philanthropist, in memory of his wife Eliza Flint Ray, with whom he fell in love when he was a penniless apprentice. Bronze reliefs show four of her favourite Charities - giving clothes to the naked, feeding the hungry, instructing the ignorant and sheltering the homeless. The figures were carved by Thomas Woolner, a pre-Raphaelite sculptor.

THE ROYAL OAK HOTEL on West Street in Wigton dates from the early 17th century and was originally a coaching inn which became known as a 'Temperance and Commercial Hotel'. Today the original archway and courtyard beyond still remain, however inside, the hotel is a pleasant combination of old and new and has a comfortable atmosphere. This is a perfect base from which to tour the area. The hotel has a licensed bar. A choice of breakfast is available every morning and packed lunches can be provided for your day out. The ten bedrooms are equipped with tea and coffee making facilities and a colour television, some have en-suite facilities. Private car parking is available in a cobbled courtyard at the rear of the hotel.

The Royal Oak Hotel, West Street, Wigton. Tel: 016973 44334

NEWTON ARLOSH, on the Solway marshes, was first established by the monks of Holm Cultram Abbey in 1307 after the old port at Skinburness had been destroyed by the sea. The village's name comes from 'the new town on the marsh'. Work on the church did not begin till 1393, but the result is one of the most delightful examples of a Cumbrian fortified church. In the Middle Ages there was no castle nearby to protect the local population from the Border raids and so a pele tower was added to the church. The narrow doorway measures 2ft 7in and the 12in, arrow slot, east window makes it the smallest in England. After the Reformation, the church became derelict but was finally restored in the 19th century. Inside, there is a particularly fine eagle lectern carved out of bog-oak.

ABBEYTOWN , as its name suggests, grew up around the 12th-century Abbey of Holm Cultram on the River Waver and many of the buildings are constructed of stone taken from the abbey when it fell into ruins. The village is small, little more than a hamlet, surrounded by ancient farms in a rolling landscape of lush meadows. Founded by Cistercians in 1150, the Abbey bore the brunt of the constant feuds between the English and the Scots. In times of peace the community prospered and soon became one of the largest suppliers of wool in the North. Edward I stayed here in 1300 and again in 1307 when he made Abbot Robert De Keldsik a member of his Council. After Edward's death the Scots returned with a vengeance and in 1319 Robert the Bruce sacked the Abbey, even though his own father, the Earl of Carrick, had been buried there 15 years earlier.

The final blow came in 1536 when Abbot Carter joined the Pilgrimage of Grace, the ill-fated rebellion against Henry VIII's seizure of Church lands and property. The rebellion was put down with ruthless brutality and the red sandstone church of St Mary survived because local people pointed out that it was the only building strong enough to provide protection against Scottish raiders. It is still the parish church and was restored in 1883, a strange yet impressive building with the original nave shorn of its tower, transepts and chancel. The east and west walls are heavily buttressed and a porch with a new roof protects the original Norman arch of the west door. Within the church buildings is a room, opened by Princess Margaret in 1973, which contains the gravestones of Robert the Bruce's father and that of Mathias and Juliana De Keldsik, relations of Abbot Robert. There are some lovely walks along the nearby River Waver which is especially rich in wildlife.

SILLOTH is an old port and a seaside resort well worth exploring. Its promenade provides wonderful views of the Solway Firth and the coast of Scotland. The town centre is made particularly attractive by thirty six acres of grassy, open space known simply as 'The Green'.

With the coming of the railways in the 1850s, Silloth came into being as a port and railhead for Carlisle. The Railway Company helped to develop the town, and had grey granite shipped over in its own vessels from Ireland to build the handsome church which is such a prominent landmark. The region's bracing air and low rainfall made Silloth a popular seaside resort. Today it remains a delightful place to stroll, to admire the sunken rose garden, the pinewoods and two miles of promenade. The 18-hole golf course was the 'home course' where Miss Cecil Leitch (1891-1978), the most celebrated woman golfer of her day, used to play. Another famous woman player was the great contralto, Kathleen Ferrier, who stayed in the town for part of her tragically short life.

SKINBURNESS was, in the Middle Ages, a lively market town and was used by Edward I in 1299 as a base for his navy when attacking the Scots. A few years later a terrible storm destroyed the town and what survived became a small fishing hamlet. It's well worth the short walk along the two mile spit of land, GRUNE POINT, the start of the Allerdale

Ramble, to view the great estuary and the beautiful, desolate expanse of marshland and sandbank. Grune Point once contained a long-vanished Roman fort, but now forms part of a designated Site of Special Scientific Interest because of the variety of its birdlife and marsh plants.

BECKFOOT is in the opposite direction from Silloth, further down the coast. At certain times and tides, the remains of a prehistoric forest can be seen on the sand-beds. To the south of the village is the site of a 2nd-century Roman fort known as 'Bibra'. According to an inscribed stone found here, it was once occupied by an Auxiliary Cohort of 500 Pannonians (Spaniards) and surrounded by a large civilian settlement. Look out for the small stream flowing into the sea which was used in World War I as a fresh water supply by intrepid German U-boats. There is also a Quaker meeting house (now a private house) and a graveyard dating from 1735.

This part of Cumbria was a Quaker stronghold in the 17th and 18th centuries and in OLD MOWBRAY, a village of whitewashed cottages two miles further south, the first Quaker marriage was held in great secrecy amongst the sandhills.

HOLME ST. CUTHBERT, a hamlet a couple of miles inland, is also known as Rowks because in the Middle Ages there was a chapel here dedicated to St Roche. The present church dates from 1845, but contains an interesting torso of a medieval knight wearing chain-mail. It was found by schoolboys on a nearby farm, the hollowed-out centre being used as a trough. It seems to be a 14th-century piece and could be a statue of Robert the Bruce's father who died at Holm Cultram Abbey. North-east of the hamlet, and enveloped among low hills, is a lovely 30-acre lake known as Tarns Dub which is a haven for birdlife.

The headland of DUBMILL POINT is popular with sea-anglers. When the tide is high and driven by a fresh westerly wind, the sea covers the road with lashing waves. Spray is often sent down the chimney of an old farm which was built on the site of a former water corn-mill belonging to the abbey of Holm Cultram.

ALLONBY, just to the south has a history as a sea-bathing resort in the 18th century and it still keeps much of its Georgian and early Victorian charm with cobbled lanes, alleyways and some interesting old houses. It was also an important centre for herring fishing and some of the old kippering houses can still be seen.

Lanes lead from here to BROMFIELD, where there was a wooden church in the 2nd century. Its stone replacement stands on the site where St. Mungo (the affectionate name for St. Kentigern) came in AD670. Close by he sank a well which is still there, capped by a stone cover, and still used by villagers for christenings.

ASPATRIA lies on the main A596 road immediately above the shallow Ellen Valley. For most visitors its main interest is the elaborate memorial fountain to 'Watery Wilfred', Sir Wilfred Lawson MP (1829-1906), a lifelong crusader for the Temperance Movement and International Peace. The much-restored Norman church is entered through a fine avenue of yew trees. It contains some ancient relics which include a 12th century font with intricate carvings, a Viking hogback tombstone and a grave cover with a pagan swastika on it. Like many other churches in the area, the churchyard contains a holy well in which it is said St Kentigern baptised his converts.

on the other side of the River Ellen, between Aspatria and Cockermouth, has particularly good views to Scotland and it is well worth visiting for the little village church of St Mary that stands on a walled mound, with a buttressed exterior, thick-walled chancel and a hagioscope.

So with Scotland in our sights, we must now leave this beautiful corner of the country and hope that you have enjoyed your "journey" with us. We are most grateful for the kindness and hospitality shown to us during our time researching the area and we are sure the places featured would be pleased if you mention that "The Hidden Places" prompted your visit.

And finally, in the words of the great Lakeland poet Wordsworth:

"Persons of pure taste throughout the whole island, who, by their visits (often repeated) to the Lakes in the North of England, testify that they deem the district a sort of national property, in which every man has a right and interest who has an eye to perceive and a heart to enjoy."

Index

225

Tourist Information Centres

ALSTON, Alston Railway Station 01434 381696

AMBLESIDE, Church Street 015394 32582

APPLEBY-IN-WESTMORLAND, Boroughgate 01768 351177

BARROW-IN-FURNESS, Duke Street 01229 870156

BOWNESS-ON-WINDERMERE, Bowness Bay, 01539 442895

BRAMPTON, Market Square 01697 73433

CARLISLE, The Old Town Hall 01228 512444

COCKERMOUTH, Market Street, Tel: (01900) 822634

CONISTON, Yewdale Road 01539 441533

EGREMONT, Main Street 01946 820693

GRANGE-OVER-SANDS, Main Street 01539 534026

GRASMERE, Red Bank Road 01539 435245

HAWKSHEAD, Main Car Park 01539 436525

KENDAL, Highgate 01539 725758

KESWICK, Market Square 01768 772645

KILLINGTON LAKE, Service Area, M6 Southbound 01539 620138

KIRKBY LONSDALE, Main Street 01524 271437

KIRKBY STEPHEN, Market Square 01768 371199

LONGTOWN, Memorial Hall 01228 791876

MARYPORT, Senhouse Street 01900 813738

MILLOM, St. Georges Road 01229 772555

PENRITH, Middlegate 01768 67466

POOLEY BRIDGE, The Square 01768 486530

RAVENGLASS, Railway Station 01229 717278

SEATOLLER, Seatoller Barn 01768 777294

SILLOTH-ON-SOLWAY, The Green 01697 331944

SOUTHWAITE, M6 Service Area 01697 473445

ULLSWATER, Main Car Park 01768 482414

ULVERSTON, County Square 01229 57120

WATERHEAD, Car Park 01539 432729

WHITEHAVEN, Market Place 01946 695678

WINDERMERE, Victoria Street 01539 446499

WORKINGTON, Washington Street 01900 602923

Visitors travelling from the south should call in at the 'Gateway to Cumbria' TIC at Pavillion Motorway Services, Forton on the M6 between Junctions 32 and 33:
FORTON, M6 Service area 01524 792181

THE HIDDEN PLACES

If you would like to have any of the titles currently available in this series, please complete this coupon and send to:
M & M Publishing Ltd
118 Ashley Road,
Hale, Altrincham, Cheshire, WA14 2UN

	Each
Scotland	
Ireland	£ 5.90 ......
Northumberland & Durham	£ 5.90 ......
The Lake District & Cumbria	£ 5.90 ......
Yorkshire and Humberside	£ 5.90 ......
Lancashire & Cheshire	£ 5.90 ......
North Wales	£ 5.90 ......
South Wales	£ 5.90 ......
The Welsh Borders	£ 5.90 ......
Somerset Avon Gloucestershire & Wiltshire	£ 5.90 ......
Thames and Chilterns	£ 5.90 ......
East Anglia (Norfolk & Suffolk)	£ 5.90 ......
The South East (Surrey, Sussex and Kent)	£ 5.90 ......
Dorset, Hampshire and the Isle of Wight	£ 5.90 ......
Heart of England	£ 5.90 ......
Devon and Cornwall	£ 5.90 ......
Set of any Five	£20.00
Total	£

Price includes Postage and Packing

NAME...

ADDRESS..

....

...............................POST CODE...................................

Please make cheques payable to: M & M Publishing Ltd

NOTES

NOTES

NOTES

NOTES

NOTES

NOTES